Craft Cocktails at Home

Offbeat Techniques, Contemporary Crowd-Pleasers, and Classics Hacked with Science

By Kevin Liu

D0094175

Copyright

ISBN-13: 978-0615766386 | ISBN-10: 0615766382

BISAC: Cooking / Beverages / Wine & Spirits

Typefaces: Adobe Garamond Pro, Century Gothic

Contents

List of Recipes

List of Interviews

How to Read This Book and Why There's No Such Thing as a "Craft" Cocktail

What is a craft cocktail, exactly? Is a Manhattan a craft cocktail? Sure, if it's made with care and properly balanced. But served in a plastic cup with months-old vermouth? Then no, I wouldn't call that a craft cocktail. How about a sugary Piña Colada? Of course not, right? Or maybe yes, since the original version was made with good rum and took months to formulate.

You can't determine whether a cocktail is "craft" based on its recipe alone. The word "craft" means that someone has spent the time and attention to create a product worth enjoying. In bartending (as in other fields), this attention is called mindfulness—mindfulness of how tastes and aromas affect each other, mindfulness of a drink's temperature and dilution, and even mindfulness of a customer's mood.

This book began as an attempt to document some of the exciting things happening with cocktails from 2008 to 2012. I was inspired by the cocktail blog of three PhD students who were thinking about drinks in ways that completely changed my view of what a cocktail was. As I started doing the research for this book, I met others, both online and in person, who shared my obsessions and passions, though not always in relation to cocktails. I realized that cocktails are just a vehicle for embracing the mindfulness it takes to execute any "craft."

I hope that you are inspired by some of the ideas in this book to explore your own craft, be that origami, fencing, or mixing drinks. And in case it ends up being the latter, please visit the companion blog to this book to share your own experiments and recipes. There, you will find updated links, raw data sets, and summaries of the latest news in cocktail culture.

Start Here

Read this book depending on what you want to get out of it:
- **If you're just starting out:** See the next chapter, "Down the Rabbit Hole" for some no-nonsense tips on getting started mixing cocktails at home. After that,

skip ahead to "How to Choose and Buy Glassware". Read through "Drinks to Convert the Cocktail Novice" and try some of the recipes. Don't be afraid to grab a few other books on cocktails—my recommendations are in the chapter titled "Find the Cocktail Recipes You Really Want" and more can be found on the book's blog.

- **Hackers and makers:** Here are the projects you'll want to try: there's a multi-purpose temperature controller, a $20 home cold-smoker, an overkill 1-micron strainer, and a beer-foamer all in the "Hardware" section. Read about carbonation in the "Drinks to Convert a Cocktail Novice" section, and check out a cool fish-tank bubble-maker in "Odds and Ends." Also, don't miss my interview with super-maker-geeks QandAbe. Some tools and purchasing options are listed throughout the text, but most are reiterated in the "Tools and Sources" section.

- **The professional bartender:** You, sir or madam, most likely know more about classic or craft cocktails than I ever will. I submit only that you take a look at the section "Foundations of Flavor" for some interesting science behind why customers like what they like. You may also want to browse the list of interviews, since although I am no expert, I managed to convince a few to speak with me.

- **The devout cocktail geek:** You've probably seen most of the info in this book in blogs and forums, so I've included a special section just for you: an annotated bibliography with dozens of books, papers, and websites for you to explore to your heart's content. You're welcome.

- **I'm just here for the buzz:** I hear ya, sister. Skip back to the list of recipes, a few pages down. Then, once you've exhausted those, I have a few tricks and hacks that will help you find more in the chapter "Find the Cocktail Recipes You Really Want".

What's Not in this Book

Journalist Malcolm Gladwell writes that it takes 10,000 hours to turn a novice into an expert, whether the skill be archery or chess. A professional bartender has the opportunity to create dozens of drinks night after night, usually tasting each one. With this experience, she gains the intuition to look at a recipe and simply *feel* how it will taste.

The home cocktail geek rarely[1] has the time or resources to develop this intuition. Since I am not and have never been a bartender, many of the recipes in this book have not been tested at a bar. Where possible, I've collected recipes from well-respected bartender friends who have been gracious enough to share their creativity.

I can't promise you'll like all the ideas and recipes in this book. But I do think you'll find:

- The tools and framework you'll need to look at a recipe and recognize whether it will have the flavor profile you're looking for.
- Step-by-step instructions on how to create your own signature cocktail, using only ingredients you already have at home.
- The scientific background for why some recipes work and how to improve others that don't.

Finally, I'm intentionally avoiding certain topics, such as centrifugation, rotary evaporation, liquid nitrogen, and distillation because it can cost thousands of dollars to apply these techniques properly and if you mess them up, you could do some serious hurt to yourself. Maybe in the next book.

WARNING: DANGER!!!

- Ethanol is no joke. It's flammable, it's a powerful solvent, and dispensed in excess, it can cause death or at least concentrated stupidity. Use with caution.
- Please do not adapt the techniques in this book to create your own home distilling rig without first consulting texts specifically written for that purpose. Done improperly, home-distilled spirits can cause sickness and death. Most states in the U.S. do not permit any sort of distillation without a permit.
- Although yeasts contribute an important part to the flavor of a spirit, other naturally occurring microbes can produce harmful toxins. See the chapter on preservation for more.

---

[1] There are, as always, exceptions...

- In this book, I advocate the use of some chemicals more often used in industry than at home. I have attempted to list specific suppliers and brands because not all products are food-safe. When a manufacturer says that something is "food-grade," they are saying that there are no harmful impurities in the product. If in doubt, contact the manufacturer.

- Many herbs and spices can be toxic in large quantities. However, to be harmed by any of the botanicals mentioned in this book, you would have to intentionally overdose. Please don't do that.

- Please do not consume any undiluted essential or fragrance oils. I recommend a minimum dilution of 1 part essential oil to 100 parts alcohol to produce an extract that can be used with cocktails. In these concentrations, most essential oils you can buy are considered Generally Recognized as Safe (GRAS) by the U.S. Food and Drug Administration (FDA).[2]

Author's Note

Parts of this book have been adapted from posts that originally appeared on http://craftcocktailsathome.com and http://sciencefare.org.

Some of the links in this book are bulky. In some cases, I've referred to a website without providing a full URL because I assume you will be able to find your way there. In either case, you can visit the blog for full URLs, they will be posted and updated there. Similarly, citations do not follow a rigorous format because this is not a scholarly work. If unclear, full citations may be requested through the blog.

This book was written and researched in the United States; as such, recommendations for where to buy tools and ingredients are based on what's available in this country. I would love to hear from you if you are outside the States and have recommendations specific to your region of the world. Contact information will be updated on the book's blog.

For more thoughts from me, turn to page 230.

---

[2] Here's a list: http://www.anandaapothecary.com/articles/essential-oils-safe-for-ingestion.html

Down the Rabbit Hole:
How to Mix Your First Drink

I'll admit: I'm targeting this book at people who are already enamored with cocktails and want to learn more about what differentiates a good drink from a great one. But if you've never mixed a drink in your life and just want to know how to get started, don't worry: I've got you covered.

The below recommendations will set you on the right track for a minimal investment. And I'm talking *really minimal*. If you're looking for some more standard recommendations, check out the section on "Tools and Sources" at the end of the book.

Really Basic Tools

I regret to admit I have used every one of these tools, at some time or another...

Instead of a Shaker
- Use a *well washed* sports-drink bottle. The plastic makes a good insulator for your hands and the wide mouth lets you add plenty of ice. The lid doubles as a decent strainer (see picture, above).

Instead of a Measuring Cup or Jigger

- Precise measures are critical to making well-balanced cocktails. Terrific options can be had for under $10. In a pinch, cut off the bottom three inches of a standard water bottle. The bottle's cap holds about 0.2 fluid ounces of liquid, but we'll round up and call it ¼ oz. for simplicity's sake. Use the bottle cap to measure out ¼, ½, ¾, 1, 1.5, and 2 oz. markings on the 3-inch portion of water bottle. Draw lines with a sharpie.

Instead of a Citrus Juicer

- Use your hands.

Instead of Going to a Bar

- Build your own. Before I even bought a bed at my last apartment, I started work on an L-Bar for my living room. It was built entirely of plywood and a scavenged table top, but it did the trick. The entire 9-foot-long monstrosity was completed for under $200. I used barplan.com—for $20, it gives you all the information you need to build a custom bar for a bachelor pad, and you can explore the forums for some higher-class designs worthy of a swank booze collection. I have no affiliation with this company.

The First Bottles

At the peak of my newfound obsession with cocktails, I would spend upwards of $300 *a month* buying obscure bottles because I had seen some recipe that called for it on a blog or in a book. Lesson learned: some spirits were meant to be forgotten. I found myself reading and rereading this paragraph written by my friend John Rutherford, hidden in his original guide on stocking one's first bar:

> **"Above all, a bar should be stocked drink by drink.** Find a cocktail you like enough to make it regularly at home, then get the Cointreau or Benedictine or rum or even absinthe necessary to make it. Put aside some money each month to get a new bottle to expand your repertoire. For instance, Steven, with his penchant for Last Words and variants thereon, might consider splurging on some Chartreuse and Maraschino liqueur. And then those drinks will cost $3 at home instead of $12 at the bar."[3]

---

[3] http://observationalgastrophysics.blogspot.com/2009/09/bar-of-ones-own.html

What if you're not even sure what drinks you like to drink?

The 9-Step Plan to Booze-Buying Success

(think of it like AA in reverse):

1. Generate a list of well-reviewed restaurants in your city. Use the local newspaper, Yelp, or some other source. Hotel concierges can be a wealth of knowledge.
2. Filter your list to include only those establishments that have a bar-seating area.
3. Grab a friend or two, and head to the bar between Tuesday and Thursday. Bartenders are more likely to have a conversation with you on these slower days when they're not swamped. Many places are closed Mondays.
4. Talk to the bartender about your likes and dislikes. Be specific, if possible. "I love the smell of caramel" works much better than "I like sugar."
5. Order a few drinks between your group and have a mini tasting party.
6. Pick out one or two of your favorites and ask the bartender for the recipe. Most bartenders are really nice and are happy to share. If they won't or can't, ask for the recipe of a "classic cocktail" similar to the drink you liked. That should be easy to agree to.
7. Look up the base spirit of your drink(s) of choice on liquor review site drinkhacker.com; choose a few highly-rated choices within your budget.
8. Visit your local spirits vendor. Try not to drop $300 in one go.
9. Mix a drink using the recipe you got from the bartender, taste, and take notes. Try varying the ingredients slightly one way or another.

Notes:

- For even more resources, I highly recommend the blog 12 Bottle Bar for a huge variety of classic cocktails using only 12 bottles of booze, and About.com cocktails for great no-nonsense guides to getting started, from glassware types to party drinks.
- Feel free to visit a cocktails-focused bar rather than a restaurant if you prefer. I recommend starting off with a restaurant bar because (1) you have the option to order food (a good choice when doing a multi-drink tasting), (2) you're more likely to get a seat at the bar, and (3) you're more likely to be able to talk to the same bartender over the course of multiple drinks.

Now that we've knocked out some of the basics, it's time to get into the...

FOUNDATIONS OF FLAVOR

My hands smelled like a mix between gasoline, flower petals, and air freshener. No matter how hard I scrubbed with soap and water, the scent persisted. It was my own stupid fault. I had seen a nondescript bottle of perfume hidden in plain sight on the sink in my mom's house. Thinking I could steal a whiff without getting any liquid to actually stick to my skin, I tentatively pressed the shiny steel button.

It's not like I have a perfume fetish. In fact, I never wear perfumes or colognes, which is part of the reason I was so intrigued. I had just finished reading Chandler Burr's *The Emperor of Scent*, a surprisingly technical exploration of the physiology of smell. My head swam with the imagined scents of ripe mangoes, bitter almonds, and black truffle. Suddenly, I craved perfume as if it were bacon.

Unfortunately, my mom's drugstore scent ended up an unpleasant first foray into the world of smell. The particles that seemed to float innocently enough through the air instantly bonded to my skin and for hours afterward they became a beacon broadcasting to the world: *don't I smell pretty?*

That first horrifying foray into smell should have scarred me for life, but one idea would continue to nag at me as I worked on this book: the cocktail's closest cousin is *perfume*. You see, perfume is nothing more than flavors dissolved in alcohol. Cocktails apply the same concept, except we experience the flavors of a cocktail primarily as taste rather than as scent.

Or do we?

The Chemistry and Physiology of Flavor

I didn't mean to start this book off with physiology and neuroscience, but some of the questions in this section, "Foundations of Flavor" are worth asking. There are very few recipes in this section, but the background information will help you understand why I came up with some of the techniques described later in the book.

Let's begin by following a sip of wine on its journey through the eyes, the nose, and the mouth.

Before the Mouth: Orthonasal Olfaction

In the wineglass, volatile aromatic compounds fill the air above the wine. These aromatics include aldehydes, ketones, and other small molecules that float around easily.

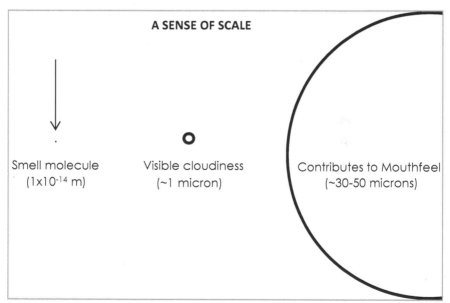

A SENSE OF SCALE

Smell molecule
(1×10^{-14} m)

Visible cloudiness
(~1 micron)

Contributes to Mouthfeel
(~30-50 microns)

This graphic is useful in this chapter, but is also relevant to the next chapter on mouthfeel and a later chapter on filtration.

When aromatic compounds enter the nose, they first pass by your standard nose hairs (the ones you clip every once in a while, hopefully) and then come into contact with specialized **olfactory cilia**, microscopic nose hairs that latch on to dust and other impurities in the air. These impurities are swept down into the mucus of the nose for later disposal. Meanwhile, smellable compounds start high-fiving with olfactory receptors.

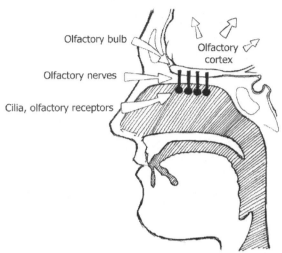

Whereas the mouth can distinguish 5-ish tastes and perhaps a few hundred dimensions of bitterness, the nose can single out tens of thousands, if not millions, of different scents.[4] There is a long and dramatic history of debate about how smell receptors function, but scientists agree that only relatively small molecules—usually organic molecules with molecular weights of less than 300—can be sensed. Everything else floats right on by.

Each cilium is covered with **olfactory receptors**. When these receptors identify a smell or group of smells, they report their findings via the **olfactory nerve** to the **olfactory bulb**, a brain structure located just above the nose and directly behind the eyes. The olfactory bulb acts as a sort of switchboard for attention. If a particular scent is deemed worthy of further investigation, its data makes its way to the **olfactory cortex**, which is just a fancy term for "a whole bunch of other parts of the brain that help to process smell."

---

[4] There are differing opinions on what the true number is; while the total combination of smell receptors that could be activated by a given smell approaches many millions, some researchers argue only around 10,000 combinations can be distinguished by the brain.

Smell is the only sense that proceeds directly to the cortex of the brain. All the other senses make a pit stop at the **thalamus**, a small structure that sits on top of the spinal cord and whose sole responsibility is to direct traffic for sensory input.

Here's an important point to remember: the olfactory bulb can decide to emphasize some scents over others, but it doesn't throw any out, whereas the thalamus literally filters sensations out, as if they never happened. For example, what does the roof of your mouth taste like? What does the texture of your chair feel like on your left thigh? Answer: probably nothing, because the thalamus ignores these mundane inputs, no matter how hard you try to focus your attention on them.

Initial Entry: Taste and the Mouth

My thanks go to John Shen, PhD candidate in neuroscience at the University of Southern California, for assistance with the following section.

While the wine is still outside the mouth, sight and smell trigger the body to prepare for a gastronomic experience. The pancreas releases digestive hormones and saliva glands release **saliva**, a salty blend of water and proteins. This means that paying attention to a drink can actually make it taste better because saliva contains **mucins**, proteins that contribute to a juicy or viscous mouthfeel (more on that in the next chapter).

Attention also amplifies perception. The conscious choice to focus on a drink triggers the brain's **prefrontal cortex** to direct the olfactory bulb and thalamus to allow more sensory input into other regions of the brain, such as the **amygdala** (the area responsible for emotional responses) and the **hippocampus** (the area responsible for forming long-term memories of experiences).

When the wine enters the mouth, the taste receptors jump into action. Taste buds are distributed around the tongue and mouth. A taste bud is an onion-shaped bundle of between 50 and 100 taste receptors. Each taste bud can contain every type of taste receptor, though the distribution of receptors varies across the mouth.

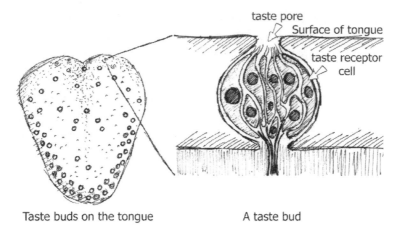

taste pore
Surface of tongue
taste receptor cell

Taste buds on the tongue   A taste bud

Most people can easily rattle off the "basic" tastes—sweet, sour, salty, and bitter. But recent research continues to challenge the notion that taste must be limited to these four dimensions. Look closely at the mechanisms of taste and it's pretty clear that our understanding of taste is far from conclusive.

Bitter. There's a physiological and evolutionary reason why a dash of bitters adds complexity to an otherwise mundane drink. In nature, bitterness often corresponds to the presence of toxins. It's no surprise then that humans have evolved dozens of taste receptors that respond to different types of bitterness, as one small taste mis-step could have spelled doom for our ancestors. It's been estimated that overlap between different receptors results in the ability to distinguish between 300 distinct forms of bitterness.

Sour. The experience of sourness has long been associated with the pH of food, where pH is a measure of the concentration of hydrogen ions in a solution. However, recent studies suggest that specific taste receptors may also play a part. I suspect this is true, as it's possible to taste the difference between citric, lactic, and malic acids, for example.

Sweet. The simplest of the tastes. In the ancestral human world, sweet = good. Try tasting the difference between pure sucrose and fructose. You can tell that one is sweeter, but that's about it.

Umami, Salt, and Mineral Channels. Specific taste receptors have been identified that bond with glutamate, the umami half of the well-known Monosodium Glutamate molecule. Glutamates are non-essential amino acids that serve as an important neurotransmitter, among other functions in the body. The sodium half of MSG and the sodium in table salt are detected through ion channels. That is, the taste receptor responsible for saltiness simply detects the presence of Na^+ (or a few similar ions, such as potassium), allows the ion through, and sends off a message letting the brain know to perceive saltiness. Recent research also points to the ability of the tongue to detect other minerals, such as calcium and magnesium. Read the chapter on water for more thoughts on that.

To learn about how tastes interact, read the chapter "How to Properly Balance a Drink: Two Approaches."

Right Back Out Again: Retronasal Smell

While your tongue is busy processing and sending the data from its army of taste receptor microprocessors up to the brain, tiny amounts of wine make their way up the nasal passage to the same olfactory receptors that first encountered the wine through orthonasal smell.

But, this second sniff is not redundant. When you first sipped the wine into your mouth, the **amylase** enzyme in your saliva quickly broke down complex carbohydrates in the wine into simple ones that volatize at body temperature. These new volatiles are detected only during retronasal smell, so the second look appears different from the first and adds more complexity to the taste experience.

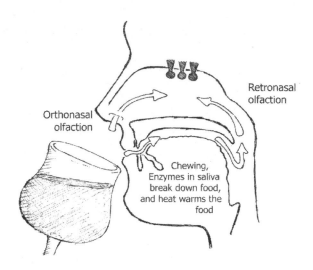

According to Gordon Shepherd in his groundbreaking book *Neurogastronomy*, **taste** is what the mouth senses through taste receptors. **Smell** is what the nose senses, either through orthonasal or retronasal olfaction. **Flavor** is the intersection of the two. And when I say intersection, I mean literally. When you sip a glass of wine or chew on a hunk of blue cheese, your brain combines the inputs from your nose and mouth into a single experience through a unique brain ability known as **synesthesia**.

Barb Stuckey, in her book *Taste: What You're Missing* argues that flavor is actually the addition of a third dimension to taste and smell: touch.

What You Need to Know about Mouthfeel and How to Recreate Lost Classics

Beef tendon has no right to be a food. Cooked slowly for hours, it transforms from a tough connective tissue into a slimy mass tasting roughly how I imagine a boiled gel insole might taste. But I love the stuff. And since beef tendon tastes like nothing, I know that the only reason I like it must be because I have an affinity for its unique texture.

If you were to order all the parts of the body by the density of the nerves found in those areas, the face (especially the lips and tongue) would rank toward the top. This is partly because human beings communicate thousands of subtle nonverbal cues through tiny movements in the facial muscles. Happily, for foodies this means that our mouths can feel tiny differences in the texture of foods.

Taste perceptions from the tongue are routed through one of two cranial nerves; front-of-mouth sensations are the domain of the **facial nerve** while back-of-mouth sensations are carried up to the **glossopharyngeal nerve**. This is where the split between taste and touch becomes apparent. All **somatosensory** inputs are processed by the **trigeminal nerve**. These include the traditional sense of touch, as well as pain, temperature, chemical irritation, and proprioception (the position of one's own body, like how far the jaw has moved to chew a bite of food).

The Dimensions of Liquid Mouthfeel

Few scientists have studied the mouthfeel of beverages because solid foods are so much more interesting from a texture standpoint. Crispness, hardness, mastication, and proprioception are some of the more studied dimensions of mouthfeel, and none of them apply to liquids. Which ones do? Below are the mouthfeel factors I think are most important to cocktails and how each can be used to tweak a drink.

Viscosity/Density: Think "thickness." Viscosity corresponds with the amount of energy required to move a physical mass through a liquid. Density is calculated by dividing a liquid's mass by its volume. While viscosity and density can be measured separately with the aid of instruments, people tend to experience the two sensations as a single parameter. For example, some powerful thickeners can transform liquid water into a paste at only a few grams per liter. The viscosity of the water changes dramatically, but its density changes only slightly. The tongue has a hard time differentiating between these two experiences; to it, the experiences are one and the same.

Creaminess/Smoothness: When you think of creaminess, I want you to think literally of cream. Cream, like any dairy product, is an emulsion of fat in water. When the globules of fat get too large, we start perceiving the emulsion as grainy or chunky—the opposite of smooth and creamy. This is what happens when cream curdles. To get a smooth and creamy drink, it's important to break up fat particles as much as possible, which can be achieved through physical agitation or the application of an emulsifier. The human tongue can only distinguish particle sizes larger than 30 microns or so. People also tend to associate increasing viscosity with increased creaminess, to a certain extent. Finally, keep in mind that fats are not the only particles that can be suspended in a liquid. Foams are emulsions of gas in liquid and they express creaminess in much the same way—smaller air bubbles means smoother mouthfeel.

Burning/Pungency/Cooling/Numbness: These are just some of the words people use to describe *chemesthesis*, a group of distinct, often irritating sensations that play an important role in taste. A number of different receptors in the tongue and mouth experience the different nuances of these inputs, the most important of which for our purposes is TRPV-1[5] because it responds directly to alcohol. Carbonation also usually falls under this category as a "tingling" sensation, though it's been shown that carbonation also triggers the same taste receptors that experience acidity. Chili peppers cause burning sensations, the Sichuan peppers in particular numb the tongue, and mint causes cooling sensations.

Oiliness: The last two dimensions are both relevant to cocktail creation and relatively little-explored. They're tricky. The standard test for gauging how oily a beverage is compares the test drink to water that has had a few drops of vegetable oil

---

[5] Transient receptor potential cation channel subfamily V member 1.

added to it. Few drinks contain enough actual oil that the oils themselves would be noticeable as a trigeminal sensation. But many cocktails certainly taste "silkier" than others.

In straight distilled spirits, a silky mouthfeel may be caused by the presence of small amounts of higher-order alcohols such as propanol, isobutanol, and methyl-butanols.[6] These alcohols contain more carbon atoms than ethanol and have a mouthfeel that approaches oil the higher order they go. Have you ever examined the "legs" that run down the sides of a whisky glass? These are the physical manifestations of the differing viscosities of all the alcohols present. But, most oily or slick mouthfeels do not come from fancy spirits; rather, they are the result of an absence of astringency.

Astringency: The mouth-puckering or "dry" sensation of astringency is caused by the binding of phenolic compounds to proteins in the mouth and saliva. The most prominent component of human saliva is mucin, a high-molecular weight protein that has high elasticity and low solubility. That is to say, the stuff is slimy. When we have a high concentration of mucin in our saliva, we perceive foods as oily or silky because our own bodies produce lubricants that mimic that mouthfeel. Saliva production is increased when we anticipate eating or when we experience particularly acidic foods (the pH of saliva is around 6; if the pH of the mouth is lowered by food, additional saliva is released to dilute the solution). Astringency also decreases when the viscosity of a liquid increases, to a certain extent.[7]

Why Does Mouthfeel Matter?

Reason #1: I hope the research presented above gives you the words you need to define the texture you're looking for in a cocktail.

Example: We typically prefer cocktails on the slightly more-viscous-than-water side. Heck, we even like straight shots like that. Remember that bottle of Bacardi you still have in the freezer? At -20°C, a common temperature for a freezer, high-

---

[6] Whisky Technology, Production, and Marketing (2003), pg 284.
[7] Chemistry of Wine Flavor (1998), 162.

proof booze has around the same thickness as a 30% sugar syrup at room temperature, or about twice the viscosity of water.

Reason #2: It's important to understand that all of the dimensions of mouthfeel are interconnected and it is impossible to change one without affecting the others.

Example: In creamy drinks, we typically like "more creamy," but we don't like it when emulsified components get too thick because then they begin to separate and "creamy" becomes "lumpy." Similarly, if emulsions are not viscous enough, they will register as "oily" instead of "creamy."

As I mentioned before, oiliness and astringency are rarely applied to cocktails (though they play an important role in both beer and wine production). But this book goes there: the chapter on "The Flip: Emulsions, With and Without Egg" is all about creamy drinks and I call for adding wine tannin directly to the Martini Sour cocktail, located in the "The Sour: Acid Alternatives to Citrus" chapter.

But enough with the technical stuff; time for some prac-app.

Gum Arabic: The Forgotten Hydrocolloid

In his seminal book, *Imbibe!*, David Wondrich prints a recipe for gum syrup, citing the work of Mr. E. Ricket and Mr. C. Thomas, English bartenders who, after traveling the world to collect a book of cocktail recipes, printed instructions for "gum syrup" under the section titled "American Cocktails." Where did Ricket and Thomas find their recipe for gum syrup? I'd ask them, but they've probably been dead for at least 100 years. The recipe they penned was published in 1871 and was only revived through the work of modern cocktail geeks/historians like Wondrich.

Gomme Syrup, 1871 Style
Inspired by The Gentleman's Table Guide, 1871

(Yields 2 cups)	Yields 5 pts
(151 g) Gum Arabic	1 lb. Gum Arabic
(120 ml) Water	1.5 pts Water
(226 g) Sugar	3 lbs Sugar
(40 ml) Water	0.5 pt Water

Heat the larger portion of the water until it boils and dissolve the gum arabic into it. Make simple syrup with the remaining sugar and water. Once the gum arabic is dissolved, combine the two liquids.

Note:
- These two recipes above are identical; in the one on the left I've simply converted the measures to produce a smaller amount. 5 pints is a lot of syrup.

What's so great about gomme syrup anyway? Back in the day, bartenders regularly used gomme in place of simple syrup. Gum arabic is special in that it acts as both a thickener and an emulsifying agent. That is, it affects two dimensions of mouthfeel — viscosity and creaminess—at the same time.

As well-known as gum syrup was 150 years ago, why is it considered an obscure ingredient today? The answer lies somewhere between the political strife in Sudan, the world's traditional exporter of gum arabic, and the development of modern **hydrocolloids**, the scientific name for thickeners and gelling agents that work in water. Today, the food industry uses combinations of hydrocolloids to replicate the characteristics of gum arabic, because these modern ingredients are cheaper and more reliable than sourcing the original stuff. In the next section we'll apply the same approach.

A Replacement for Gum Arabic

The main problem with using gum arabic today is its price. Just look at the amounts called for in the traditional recipe, above. The sources I've found for food-grade gum arabic[8] charge about $50/kilogram. How much would 2 cups of gomme syrup cost? About $7.50: a price impractical for most people. Time to find a replacement.

When I set out to recreate gomme syrup, I expected it to be much more difficult than it was. I tried over a dozen different combinations of hydrocolloids, but one of the simplest ended up being the best.

<u>Gomme Syrup, Modern Style</u>

Yields 2 cups
20 g Gum Arabic
10 g Egg White Powder
.24 g Xanthan Gum
220 ml Water
226 g Sugar

Heat the water and dissolve the gum arabic and xanthan into it. Let cool to just warmer than room temperature, then add sugar and egg white powder. Stir to combine. Allow to rest for 2-3 hours before use, as the syrup will thicken over time.

Notes:

- Any syrup can be made as a gomme syrup, but keep in mind that the acidity and sugar content of fruits can affect both viscosity and foam stability. If in doubt, use the same scaling of gum arabic, but halve the concentrations of xanthan and egg white powder, taste, then add more of those ingredients as necessary.

---

[8] Gum arabic is also commonly used in painting and photography. I would not recommend using product meant for these uses in cocktails.

- Store in the refrigerator and use within a week, or try some of the preservation techniques discussed in the chapter titled "Preservation" in the Basic Mixers section.

- For sources of xanthan gum, gum arabic, and egg white powder, look under "modernist ingredients" in the "Tools and Sources" chapter at the end of the book.

Why does this work?

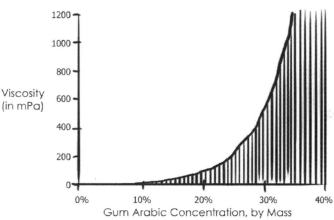

Viscosity (in mPa) vs. Gum Arabic Concentration, by Mass

Gum arabic serves two functions in cocktails: emulsification and thickening. Thickening was the easy part. The above graph shows that at the concentrations typically used in gomme syrup, gum arabic contributes a viscosity of around 1000 mPa (milli Pascals). Xanthan gum easily replicates this same viscosity with only a 0.1% concentration by mass.[9] Xanthan also has the added benefits of maintaining its thickening properties in the presence of acids, like lemon juice.

Emulsification is slightly more tricky. Gum arabic needs to be used in a 1:1 gum:oil ratio in order to achieve a silky mouthfeel.[10] I chose to keep some gum arabic in this formulation because it imparts a unique taste and color, but I doped the emulsifying power of the mix with egg white powder, a much stronger emulsifier. With that being said, egg white powder gives a lighter, more airy texture than gum arabic alone. Feel free to tweak as needed.

---

[9] Figure adapted from Phillips and Williams, Handbook of Hydrocolloids (2009), pg. 265
[10] McNamee et al., *Emulsification and microencapsulation properties of gum arabic* (1998).

Why Some People Hate the Taste of Alcohol and What You Can Do About It

I have a friend named Wes who cannot stand the taste of alcohol. At all. And I know it's not his fault. He's always a good sport, tasting every single drink I've made for him. Each time, he smiles, as if confident this time, this drink, he'll find something he'll genuinely enjoy and know exactly what to order at bars forever.

For me, it's like watching a car wreck in slow motion. I carefully study his face, looking for a sign, the slightest hint of a smile that indicates he's pleased, satisfied, or at least indifferent. But, every time it ends the same. Wes's face tightens with disgust, his eyes squint, and his tongue hangs limp from his defeated mouth.

Wes drinks Bud Lime and Corona. I drink the leftovers of Wes's cocktails. Once in a while, I'll mix up something exceptionally light and he'll happily accept a glass in the privacy of the home bar, knowing he'll never be able to bring himself to ask for an Amaretto Sour or a Dark and Stormy (hold the stormy) in public. Poor Wes.

Taste and Learning

Humans have enjoyed alcohol since 8000 B.C., but a few thousand years is probably too little time to evolve any sort of biological preference for alcohol.[11] Fortunately, we are very good at passing along our taste aversions and preferences through cultural and subconscious cues.

What if the only reason I think alcohol tastes good is because people enjoy getting drunk and somehow that drug reliance has translated into a learned preference for ethanol? Would cocktails objectively "taste" better if they were all alcohol-free?

In 2000, Dr. Anna Scinska and five of her colleagues at the University of Warsaw explored how people experience the flavor of alcohol. Dr. Scinska recruited 20 volunteers to taste small squirts of various concentrations of ethanol and describe its

---

[11] Although my friend Carolyn Tepolt, an evolutionary biologist, assures me that it is possible.

taste. Every single test subject said that ethanol tasted bitter, but many also described ethanol as tasting sweet.

In the second part of Dr. Scinska's experiment, the test subjects were invited back to refine their descriptions. When subjects tasted a 10% ethanol solution, they found it tasted most similar to a mixture of 3% sucrose and 0.005% quinine—slightly sweet and slightly bitter.[12]

In a separate study in 2004, then graduate student Sarah Lanier of the University of Connecticut noticed a link between two variables within her 49 test subjects: (1) whether they were "supertasters," —people sensitive to a specific type of bitterness— and (2) how much alcohol they consumed.

Lanier discovered that people who found scotch less bitter and more sweet drank more alcohol, but that similar perceptions about beer's bitterness had no impact. This was because high-proof drinks triggered intense sensations of bitterness in supertasters while the bitterness of beer (imparted by hops, not distilled alcohol) did not. The two types of bitterness were perceived differently.[13]

The takeaway: while many people find beer unappealingly bitter, they seem to be able to overcome that taste aversion, probably as a result of social pressure. But supertasters simply could not stand Scotch.

Aha! Now I understood why Wes could stomach some light beers, but struggled with sweet cocktails. He had probably overcome the bitterness of beer through social pressure and acquired tolerance to aversion, but the whole point of a craft cocktail is to use different strong liquors in harmony. You want to taste the alcohol. And that taste was torture for Wes.

---

[12] Scinska et al, *Bitter and sweet components of ethanol taste in humans (2000).*
[13] Lanier, Hayes, and Duffy, *Sweet and bitter tastes of alcoholic beverages mediate alcohol intake in of-age undergraduates (2005).*

What About the Burning Taste of Booze?

My friend Naveen Sinha is a physicist at Harvard who spends far too much of his free time thinking about cocktails. He once asked for my input for an article on cocktail science he was writing for Physics World.

The one question that eluded him was: what causes the burning sensation of alcohol?

I posed the question to the question and answer site Quora and after a few months got a well-researched, thorough response from a medical student named Jae Won Joh. Here's a short excerpt from that response:

> The answer is not simple, unfortunately, and it's actually a bit difficult to pinpoint. Let's go through some of the research I've been able to dig up.
>
> **Layman's summary up till 2002:** we thought ethanol was just messing with nerves, but apparently there's this special receptor that it wreaks hell on, and it just so happens to be the receptor for capsaicin, which causes the burning associated with spicy food. Innnnnteresting. Veeeeery interesting...
>
> **Layman's summary up till 2009:** we know now about alcohol and capsaicin, but it's apparent that alcohol has other taste pathways as well, possibly involving sweetness. It may even involve something else as well, given that you can still get a mouse to hate alcohol even if it doesn't have the capsaicin receptor.

Basically, what Joh summarized was that ethanol seems to trigger a pathway that is also responsible for the burning sensation you get from eating spicy foods and, importantly, that ethanol reduces the temperature at which the pain gets triggered.

I knew from previous research that there is only one way to build up a tolerance to spicy food: eat more spicy food. What if sensitivity to alcohol works in a similar fashion? The anecdotal evidence from dozens of bartenders confirms that people who drink a lot develop a taste tolerance to alcohol—it takes stronger and stronger drinks over time to generate the same amount of tingle.

How to Deal with Different Types of Drinkers

Everyone knows that flavor preferences vary greatly between people, but I had no idea ethanol could deliver such a complex range of pleasurable and unpleasurable flavors to different tasters. How a person experiences alcohol depends on his or her genetics, social/cultural influences, and tolerance built up over time. Rather than go into all the takeaways, I've organized some advice for dealing with different types of drinkers in the handy-dandy flowchart on the next page.

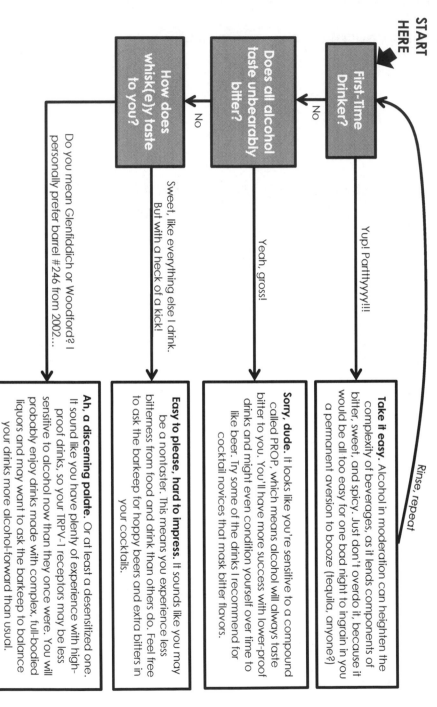

START HERE

First-Time Drinker?

Yup! Partthyyy!!!

Take it easy. Alcohol in moderation can heighten the complexity of beverages, as it lends components of bitter, sweet, and spicy. Just don't overdo it, because it would be all too easy for one bad night to ingrain in you a permanent aversion to booze (tequila, anyone?)

Rinse, repeat

No

Does all alcohol taste unbearably bitter?

Yeah, gross!

Sorry, dude. It looks like you're sensitive to a compound called PROP, which means alcohol will always taste bitter to you. You'll have more success with lower-proof drinks and might even condition yourself over time to like beer. Try some of the drinks I recommend for cocktail novices that mask bitter flavors.

No

How does whisk(e)y taste to you?

Sweet, like everything else I drink. But with a heck of a kick!

Easy to please, hard to impress. It sounds like you may be a nontaster. This means you experience less bitterness from food and drink than others do. Feel free to ask the barkeep for hoppy beers and extra bitters in your cocktails.

Do you mean Glenfiddich or Woodford? I personally prefer barrel #246 from 2002...

Ah, a discerning palate. Or at least a desensitized one. It sound like you have plenty of experience with high-proof drinks, so your TRPV-1 receptors may be less sensitive to alcohol now than they once were. You will probably enjoy drinks made with complex, full-bodied liquors and may want to ask the barkeep to balance your drinks more alcohol-forward than usual.

How to Properly Balance a Drink:
Two Approaches

Much of what makes a cocktail "craft" boils down to balance. A cocktail crafted by a clear-headed, detail-oriented and experienced bartender will inevitably taste better than the same recipe handled by a lackadaisical noob. In conversations with bartenders, I've heard time and again that balance depends on dozens of factors it would be pointless to quantify in a book. The temperature and humidity of a room, the warmth of a man's hands versus those of a woman, the quality of citrus fruit being used, are all just a few of the confounding variables a bartender has to track and manage.

Approach #1: Mindfulness

In the latter part of this chapter, I offer a few basic tips on how to balance drinks, based on the scientific literature. But those cold facts tell only half the story. The other half is mindfulness, an incredibly simple yet enormously powerful way of perceiving the world. I'll let a true practitioner explain.

Dushan Zaric on Mindful Bartending

Dushan Zaric is the bartender and co-owner of Employees Only and Macao Trading Co. in New York City. He co-authored the book <u>Speakeasy: The Employees Only Guide to Classic Cocktails Reimagined</u>.

You practice yoga and mindfulness. Has that improved your ability to fine-tune cocktails?

I definitely think so. You know, it's no secret that people who are more content with their situation are just more attractive to be around. For you to begin to see the benefits, you need to be practicing for a while and understand how that changes your life. A content person is able to focus a different kind of attitude when they are mixing cocktails.

Read more about The Institute for Mindful Bartending, an initiative started by Gaz Regan, Aisha Sharpe and Dushan.[14]

---

[14] http://www.ardentspirits.com/ardentspirits_old/Cocktails/1B20110110.html

You've written about the three levels of balance. Can you explain?

What you want is a three-dimensional cocktail. A cocktail is like a book—it has to have a beginning, an exciting middle part or development, and it has to have a surprising or logical finish. In the end, the reader needs to want to keep reading and the customer needs to want to take another sip.

How do you know when you've succeeded?

In the end, it's not the cocktail that matters. What does is that the person drinking the cocktail wants to finish it and they want to come back—not because of the cocktail, but because of the good times they remember while they were at your bar.

I always ask my bartenders to put themselves into the guest's position and to think about how many extraordinary bars that customer has been to in their life and how many extraordinary cocktails they have tried. And then I ask them: How many of those places and drinks do you think that customer really remembers? What's going to make your bar memorable?

Research shows that people's genetics affect how they perceive flavors. How do you deal with individual taste preferences?

Well, a few things to remember: generally, ladies have a more sensitive palate. It's a proven fact that one in three women are supertasters, whereas only one in ten men is a supertaster. So what does that really mean? That means that women will be more sensitive to bitter flavors. For this reason, women tend to gravitate toward the style of sweet, sour, and lighter cocktails.

But the other part of it is that bartenders have to be like marriage counselors. Marriage counselors always advise couples to practice active listening, to really hear your partner. In a hospitality environment, I actually very strongly suggest a similar approach, because the moment you stop talking to yourself and you really hear what the customer is saying, you become able to help them get what they want. If, on the other hand, you are projecting your ideas about what it is they should drink, there will be a miscommunication and the customer will get the short end of the exchange.

You make a lot of classic cocktails, but you like to tweak the ratios just slightly. How did you come up with your preferred recipes?

Jay Kosmas [co-author of *Speakeasy*] and I, we basically experimented. One of the problems we came across was that while many of the ingredients used 100 years ago are still available today, they often taste very different now than they most likely did in the past.

Let's just talk about whiskey for an example. Whisky was bottled pre-prohibition at a standard 50% ABV, or 100 proof. There was no such thing as 80-proof whiskey, though that's what dominates the majority of bottlings today. So right there you see why we can't just duplicate classic recipes without some modification. If you were to use an 80-proof spirit in a cocktail where a 100-proof spirit was originally called for, the foundation of your drink will not be able to carry the other ingredients properly.

Another example is fortified wines or sherry or madeira. Today they taste completely different from how they did 100 years ago. Some of them are more colorful and full of chemicals. Some of them are made with artificial additives for flavor. Some of them, on the other hand, are less colorful.

As a bartender, you have to know your ingredients, not just be able to read a label. If a musician goes in to a studio to record, he looks at all the equipment; I taste all the bottles behind my bar.

Do you think that's why bartenders have been so anti-dilution over the last few years? Because the whiskey we have today just isn't strong enough?

Definitely—dilution is important to get the right balance in the cocktail. Actually, I also think the trend of low-sugar cocktails is a little bit short-sighted. You know, sugar in cocktails is like salt and pepper in cooking. It amplifies the flavors and brings the whole thing into balance.

Approach #2: Taste Mixtures and Suppression

Up until 2010, the academic literature on how the basic tastes affect each other dealt primarily with binary taste interactions—that is, how salt affects bitterness, how sugar affects sourness, etc. But in 2010, Barry Green and four of his colleagues and students at the Yale-affiliated John B. Pierce Laboratory in New Haven, CT set out to systematically test every possible combination of the basic tastes.[15] They recruited 35 participants from the Yale campus and subjected each person to two series of experiments.

Before conducting their experiments, the researchers did some preliminary runs using the general Labeled Magnitude Scale[16] to produce four taste samples of roughly equal intensity:

1. Sweet: 0.56M Sucrose
2. Salty: 0.32M Table Salt
3. Sour: 10mM Citric Acid
4. Bitter: 0.18mM Quinine Sulfate

I've reproduced the values Dr. Green and team came up with here to highlight the difference in intensities of these basic tastes. Notice how much more powerful quinine sulfate has than sucrose. Here's how this looks visually:

---

[15] Umami was omitted because people generally have difficulty isolating it in taste tests and because it's believed to interact with other tastes the same way salt does, as the two share a sodium ion in their structures.

[16] The scale asks respondents to categorize a taste as "no sensation", "barely detectable", "weak", "moderate", "strong", "very strong", or "strongest imaginable sensation" and associates these subjective ratings with empirically-established numerical magnitudes.

Solutions of Equal Intensity

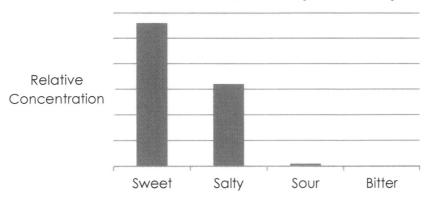

Relative
Concentration

Sweet   Salty   Sour   Bitter

The researchers gave every possible mixture of these equalized solutions to their subjects. Their results follow.

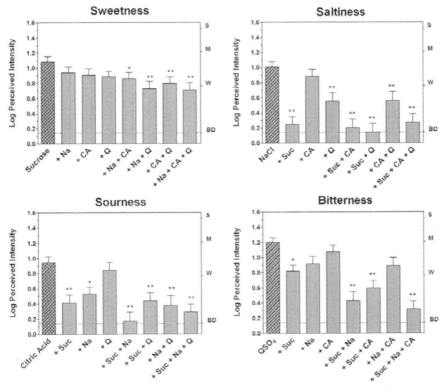

Legend: BD = Barely Detectable, W = Weak, M = Moderate, S = Strong

The takeaways I got from Green and team's work that are most relevant to cocktail balancing:

- **Sugar dominates.** Sweetness is the most difficult taste to suppress. Saltiness is the easiest.

- **1 + 1 < 2.** Notice how the intensities decrease from left to right as new tastes are mixed in. This means that mixing the basic tastes generally has a suppressive, not an additive effect—which is totally contradictory to common sense.

- **Synergy.** To balance an overly sour cocktail, adding sugar helps, but sugar and salt together have a much larger effect.

- **Bitters "round out" a drink.** Consider that a tiny amount of quinine was evaluated to be equivalent in intensity to a moderate sucrose solution (0.56M sucrose vs. 0.18mM QSO_4, a difference of over 3000 times!). Since the experimental evidence shows that bitterness can suppress all the other tastes, it's reasonable to suppose a "dash" of bitters helps to "round out" an otherwise harsh cocktail.

Here's one more interesting chart from the same paper:

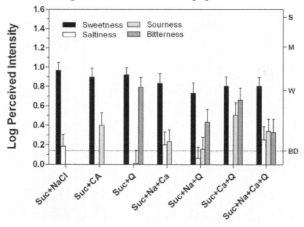

Why is this chart important?

- **Salt = magical fairy dust.** When you add sourness or bitterness to a sweet solution, the components suppress each other. That is, the result mixture tastes less sweet and less bitter or sour than the tastes would alone. But add salt to the mix and the sour or bitter flavors are suppressed significantly, while sweetness decreases only slightly. At the same time, saltiness is only barely detectable. Combine these results with other published papers on salt and suppression of bitterness[17] and the takeaway is that a undetectable amount of salt can be used to suppress bitter and sour flavors and essentially amplify sweetness.[18]

Dr. Green's paper only tells part of the story. I managed to catch him on the phone, and here's what he had to say:

Barry Green on Taste Suppression, Chemesthesis, and the Dominance of Sucrose

Dr. Green is the Director of the John B. Pierce Laboratory, where his work spans topics in taste, chemesthesis and oral somatosensation.

Your paper shows that mixing the basic tastes results in mutual suppression. Is that what's happening when a few drops of salt solution in a cocktail seems to result in a "rounder" drink?

Maybe. You see, my research dealt with suprathreshold interactions, that is, what happens when you mix tastes that can be clearly tasted by the subject. When you add a few drop of salt to a drink, that's a subthreshold interaction—the salt does something to the taste of the cocktail, but you won't be able to taste the saltiness.

It's important to remember that suprathreshold or threshold interactions do not necessarily predict what happens at subthreshold, though other published literature does show the effect you described.

You mentioned "subthreshold" and "suprathreshold". Are there established threshold values for each of the basic tastes?

Yes and no. In the medical literature, the terms are meant to describe the literal firing of a neuron in response to a stimulus. But our sense of taste is more complicated than that. A few drops of salt might be subthreshold in a cocktail, but those same two drops in a glass of water would be easy to taste.

---

[17] Breslin and Beauchamp, *Salt enhances flavour by suppressing bitterness (1997)*.

[18] Check out http://betacocktails.com/archives/544 for a mind-blowing example of what salt can do in cocktails.

Taste and taste interactions occur mostly at the perceptual level: our brains take input from our receptors and use those individual colors to paint a full picture. But we don't see blue or red individually—all we perceive is purple.

You know, mixture interactions are really important, and the reason that there is so little on it in the scientific literature is because it's so difficult to study; experiments are complicated. I had to spend a long time developing and validating what I call the labeled magnitude scale, a tool that allows researchers to assess how a taste is perceived by a subject—not just what chemical reactions are happening on the tongue.

I understand that taste is only one component of flavor—aroma and chemesthesis (the feel or irritation component of food) also play a roll. Do these components also suppress each other?

I've actually done work on both. Let's talk about aroma first. The literature is pretty clear on the fact that many aromas can heighten the perception of tastes, be that due to increased saliva flow or selective attention. Dr. Juyun Lim and I did some experiments that showed that sweet tastes can actually enhance the perception of retronasal smell as well.[19]

We were surprised in the beginning because we were using citrol, a lemon odor. But when we added citric acid (a key flavor of lemon) to that aroma, it did not enhance it. But adding sucrose to it did, and adding both citric acid and sucrose to the aroma enhanced it as well, though the enhancement did not appear to be significantly greater than what we observed with sucrose alone. We're not entirely sure why the enhancement happens only in these situations just yet, but it definitely appears that something interesting is happening!

---

[19] Green et al., *Enhancement of retronasal odors by taste (2012).*

And how about chemesthesis? Can taste suppress chemesthetic stimuli?

The classic chemesthetic components used in research are ethanol, capsaicin, and mustard oil. There is a small literature studying these ingredients. It's actually rather confusing, but to sum it all up, there appear to be weak interactions in both directions. And that was a surprise, because the researchers who originally looked at this thought there would be huge suppression of taste, since when people eat spicy foods, they tend to say they can't taste anything—that all they taste is the burn of the pepper.

But if you actually work in the normal range of intensities of the foods that we would typically eat, capsaicin does not actually have a strong suppressive effect on taste. The one exception to this general finding? Sweetness can significantly suppress the burn of capsaicin, as was just reported in a new paper in the journal Physiology and Behavior.[20]

I have this theory that because alcohol triggers the same receptors as capsaicin, people will similarly become conditioned to it over time. What do you think?

Well, capsaicins and other vanillins have a clear ability to desensitize the TRPV-1 receptor (TRPV-1), though that mechanism is above my head. But I know that it happens very quickly. Give someone just 10-15 exposures to capsaicin, come back in 15 minutes and the receptors are significantly less sensitive to capsaicin.

But that doesn't happen with alcohol. So even though alcohol stimulates the same receptors, it doesn't seem to have the same biophysical effects on the receptors. There's probably a long-term habituation to the irritancy of ethanol, but the receptors themselves are probably not physically desensitized.

---

[20] Schöbel et al., *Sweet taste and chorda tympani transection alter capsaicin-induced lingual pain perception in adult human subjects (2012).*

But you're saying that people who enjoy spicy foods might become desensitized to alcohol?

Yes, and I actually studied that. There have been many studies done on cross-desensitization of other irritants by capsaicin. And ethanol would be included in that category. In fact, in large quantities and over time, eating a lot of capsaicin will completely knock out a significant portion of the heat- and chemical-sensitive receptors in the mouth, completely changing how a person perceives foods—including alcohol.

Dr. Green theorizes in his paper that perhaps sweetness suppresses the other tastes the most strongly because humans have evolved to value calories (sugar) over potential hazards (bitterness/sourness). So I posed the question: why, then, would something like pure bitterness suppress sourness? Green had no answer, saying only that sometimes scientific observations are made that cannot be easily explained.

Yet any decent cook will tell you: fill a dish with too many ingredients and those elements will "muddy" the flavor of the finished product. Contrary to common sense, the brain seems to *reduce* perceived complexity as recipes become more complex. We've already talked about how this happens with basic tastes; but the phenomenon occurs with aroma as well.[21] The question then becomes: at what point do additional components in a dish or drink cease to add complexity? When does marginal benefit begin to go negative? As Dr. Green noted, more research is needed.

---

[21] Weiss, Snitz, and Yablonka, *Perceptual convergence of multi-component mixtures in olfaction implies an olfactory white (2012)*.

BASIC MIXERS

In this chapter, I'll show you how to make better versions of mixers you already know and love and point out where you can buy the ones it makes more sense to buy.

Let's start with a list of common non-alcoholic mixers. It's not conclusive by any means and not every home bar needs all the ingredients found here, but it's a start.

Juices	Sodas
Citrus Juices (p. 65)	Club Soda/Seltzer (p. 132)
Cranberry Juice	Tonic Water (p. 142)
Apple Juice	Ginger Beer
Pineapple Juice	Ginger Ale (p. 137)
	Cola
	Lemon-Lime Soda

Syrups	Others
Simple Syrup (p. 82)	Bitters (p. 168)
Gomme Syrup (p. 30)	Cream
Honey	Spritzes (p. 71)
Fruit Syrups (p. 103)	Saline Solution
Grenadine (p. 124)	Fresh Fruit
Orgeat (p. 225)	Fresh Herbs
	Coconut Crème (229)

Transform Tap Water into Magical Alpine Fairy-Water

STOP. Walk over to your sink, pour yourself a glass of water straight from the tap. Taste it. Does it taste delicious? Like fairies extracted dew out of fresh mountain grasses and carried the droplets in tiny hydrophobic blankets to your glass? Then skip this section. You have no reason to start messing around with your water.

The U.S. Environmental Protection Agency (EPA) actually maintains more stringent requirements for tap water than the Food and Drug Administration (FDA) imposes for bottled water, so if your tap water ain't broke, you might do more harm than good trying to fix it. BUT if your tap water—like mine—tastes like you're licking a cast iron skillet with every sip, read on and I'll show you how to recreate alpine fairy-water out of normal tap. [22]

Myth: Water should taste like nothing.[23]
This shouldn't really come as a surprise to you, but bottled water manufacturers are lying to you. They promote the myth that bottled water is "pure" and that pure water, free from im"pure"-ities, tastes better.

Ask anyone who's spent time in a chemistry lab: distilled water tastes nasty. It suffers from two major problems: (1) when air is removed from water, it tastes "flat" and (2) completely deionized and demineralized water is much more able to react with its environment, so it quickly picks up the taste of whatever it's touching: typically plastic or the chemicals on paper cups (gross).

It's not surprising that the most delicious waters in the world all contain significant amounts of minerals and oxygen. Consider what happens in nature: rain falls on a

---

[22] I tested my tap water and got a reading of 300 ppm total dissolved solids.

[23] Actually, saliva should taste like nothing, because it is constantly in our mouths so we are completely taste-adapted to it. Saliva has a pH of about 6.0 and contains a high concentration of electrolytes (minerals) as well as mucil, which provides a slippery mouthfeel. So water that's high in electrolytes, with a pH of about 6.0 should taste like nothing.

fairy-mountain. Let's assume it's pure at this point. As the water runs down alpine mountain fairy-streams, it passes over rocks and picks up dissolved minerals like calcium, sodium, potassium, and magnesium. And since oxygen is lighter than carbon dioxide, more oxygen gets dissolved in water than carbon dioxide at high fairy-altitudes.

These facts are not lost on bottled water manufacturers. Read the fine print on your favorite plastic hydration source, and notice how many of them contain minerals in addition to water. Most natural spring waters contain anywhere from 50 to 300 mg/l of stuff other than water, known in the industry as "total dissolved solids," or TDS. Any water with TDS over 250 can be marketed as "mineral water" in the United States.

The United Kingdom even requires bottled water to contain minerals –

> *"under the UK Bottled Waters Regulations 2007 any bottled water that has been softened or desalinated must contain a minimum of 60 mg/L calcium hardness."*[24]

When you start dealing with the mass production of water, consistent quality becomes a concern. It's often easier for industry types to totally distill water and add minerals back into it rather than design filtration processes to produce a specific water profile. This process is called **remineralization** (more on this later).

Myth: All bottled waters taste the same.
In 2001, ABC's *Good Morning America* program conducted a blind taste test of tap versus bottled waters. Of the four waters tasted, 45% (the largest group) preferred New York City tap water over bottled brands.

But what if ABC just got lucky? Tap water can taste great if it comes from a good source and has been properly treated. But it can also easily pick up off tastes along the way from the reservoir to the faucet. New York tap water might start off great

---

[24] Ashurst and Hargitt, Soft drink and fruit juice problems solved (2009), pg. 122.

at the treatment facility, but the pipes at your house might be contributing metallic or organic off-flavors. Gross.

Fast forward ten years. In 2009, the investigative journalism organization *Mother Jones* ran a piece on Fiji bottled water that examined everything about the product from the socio-economic impact the product has had on the small island of Fiji to the brand's claims that each plastic bottle actually *reduces* carbon footprint.

As part of the research for the article, editor Jen Quraishi conducted a taste test of popular bottled waters using 10 tasters. The results? Volvic mineral water, Whole Foods Electrolyte Water, and unfiltered San Francisco tap came in 1-2-3, out of ten contenders.

Then, in 2011, the online current affairs Magazine *Slate* conducted their own blind taste-test of the four most popular bottled waters in the the United States. In their test, not only could the 11-member tasting panel easily differentiate between bottlings, they all clearly disliked tap water and there was a clear winner at the end of the experiment: SmartWater.

Reverse Engineering the Best-Tasting Waters

I took a look at how each of the bottled waters that dominated these two taste tests are made and made a startling discovery. Both the Whole Foods and SmartWater brands unabashedly admit they contain nothing more than purified tap water, re-mineralized with a blend of minerals.

Luckily for me, inquisitive internet-dwellers had already taken the liberty of contacting both Glaceau (the makers of SmartWater) and Whole Foods to ascertain their mineral formulas. Glaceau happily obliged, as did Whole Foods, though the Whole Foods rep cited a total 3000 ppm mineral content that seemed totally off. So I bought a bottle of each and checked the numbers. Here's all the available data, combined:

	SmartWater[25]	Whole Foods
Sodium Bicarbonate	-	Yes, unknown amt
Calcium Chloride	10mg	Yes, unknown amt
Magnesium Chloride	15mg	Yes, unknown amt
Potassium Bicarbonate	10mg	-
Total Dissolved Solids	35ppm	35ppm[26]

So in summary, two of the best-tasting brands of bottled water as judged in a blind tasting contained remarkably similar amounts and (probably) ratios of minerals.

And they're easy to recreate at home, too. Here are some recipes for water. Ridiculous? If you think so, you may want to stop this book reading here. It only gets more ridiculous.

Homemade Electrolyte (Fairy) Water

1 L Tap Water
10 g Homemade Electrolyte Concentrate (below)

Use a reverse osmosis or ZeroWater® filter to produce zero TDS water. Distilled should work too. If in doubt, test your "0 TDS water" with a TDS meter. Add the homemade electrolyte concentrate and shake violently.

---

[25] Original data: http://loewald.com/blog/?p=240

[26] Online sources said 3000 ppm, which is redonculous, so I measured it. My TDS meter read 35 ppm. But a Whole Foods rep did confirm the actual minerals. Original data here: https://getsatisfaction.com/wholefoods/topics/what_are_the_electrolyte_amounts_in_the_365_el ectrolyte_water

```
Homemade Electrolyte Concentrate

1 L Tap Water
1.50 g Magnesium Chloride
1.00 g Sodium Bicarbonate
1.00 g Calcium Chloride

Use a reverse osmosis or ZeroWater® filter to produce zero TDS water. Combine.
The mixture will stay cloudy for a while after you add the minerals, though it
should clear up in time.
```

Notes:

- Use this concentrate so you don't have to measure out 10 mg of minerals at a time. That would be annoying.

- Sodium bicarbonate is nothing more than baking soda. Potassium bicarbonate can be substituted for people who are sensitive to sodium. Potassium bicarbonate is available through beer and wine homebrew stores.

- Calcium chloride is used both for beer/winemaking and in modernist cooking. Visit retailers who specialize in those ingredients for purchasing options.

- Magnesium Chloride is available as a dietary supplement. One product I found contained 66.5 mg per 2.5 ml serving, which means you would need 5.7 mL or just over a tsp per liter of water to make Electrolyte Concentrate.

- Avoid mineral tablets, as these contain binders and anti-caking agents that can affect flavor.

What Makes Water Taste Good?

With the exception of magnesium, all of the ions listed in the table above appear in significant amounts in human saliva. However, our saliva's composition doesn't at all mirror the ratios presented here. Beyond this simple observation I can only speculate as to why this particular blend of minerals in this concentration tastes especially good.

One possible explanation may lie in total dissolved solids. I found the following information on a forum post at Home-Barista.com.[27] It quotes the Specialty Coffee Association of America's (SCAA) Water Quality Handbook:

The test methodology was blind tasting by six tasters at the SCAA Lab in Long Beach. From page 31:

"In a tasting conducted by the Technical Standards Committee of the SCAA, coffee was brewed with different levels of TDS to determine if significant flavor differences existed and how much difference actually existed. ... The same coffee, grind, and brewer were used and the same standard combination of minerals was used. The only difference was the concentration of the minerals in the brewing water. The first tasting was conducted using three water samples: one contained TDS at a level of 45 mg/L, one at 150 mg/L, and one at 450 mg/L. The coffee that was brewed with 150 mg/L water was chosen as far superior by all who judged the coffee.

A second tasting was conducted using 125 mg/L, 150 mg/L, and 175 mg/L samples to determine if minor variations in water quality would have an effect on flavor and extraction. The minor changes in the TDS of water were unanimously discernible by the panel. Acid and body balances were perceived to be off at both 125 mg/L and 175 mg/L TDS, and the 150 mg/L TDS brew was rated superior."

So the coffee geeks seem to observe that the level of total dissolved solids is more important than anything else, with no concern as to *which* solids are actually present. This didn't make sense to me, so I reached out to a chemical engineer to find out more:

---

[27]http://www.home-barista.com/knockbox/tds-water-softening-scaa-water-quality-handbook-t14678.html

54

Joe McDermott on the Taste Chemistry of Water

Joe is a chemical engineer and a postdoctoral fellow at Harvard University.

We got in touch because I heard your research area was in water. Tell me about that.

Sort of—I'm a chemical engineer by trade and my PhD thesis in Chemistry focused on colloidal particles in aqueous systems (the study of tiny stuff dispersed in liquids). So I know a little bit about water chemistry, but it's really exciting to be talking about it from the perspective of taste.

You've read through my ideas about making water taste better—what's your professional opinion?

What makes water taste good is a really interesting question. From my understanding of taste receptors, our taste buds are only set up to accept very specific tastes, like sodium chloride for salt or acids for sour.

I think you're right that mineral content is important, but I'm not sure why from a taste perspective. My gut instinct is that the cation portion of the mineral (the positively charged half) has less to do with taste than the anion side. If you look at the periodic table, a lot of the commonly found mineral cations show up really close to each other. There aren't that many chemical reactions I can think of where $Ca+$ can't simply be replaced with $Mg+$, for example.

Anions, on the other hand, can vary greatly in structure and complexity. They're often structured organic molecules. Think about MSG—monosodium glutamate. The anion half is glutamic acid, an important amino acid that serves as a neurotransmitter and has the chemical formula $C_5H_9NO_4$.

Why do you think ion concentration is important?

I work in a world where I need to know how much dissolved ionic material there is in a solution. It matters a lot more than the total dissolve mass because when ions dissolve in water, they change the charge of the water itself, which then changes how particles dispersed in the water behave. In the lab, we deionize our water to ensure. But if we get really good deionized water and let it sit out on the counter, it will measure out to 5.6 pH (relatively acidic). That's because atmospheric CO_2 dissolves really readily in water.

So, does that mean that most water will turn acidic if it's left out for a long time?

I haven't tested this in the lab, but I would think so. In fact, that's probably one reason why you see sodium bicarbonate (baking soda) or other bicarbonate minerals added to bottle water. Bicarbonates act as a pH buffer—that is, they make it so that it would require more CO_2 to dissolve in the water before it actually became acidic. Think of it as insurance for nice-tasting water.

Here are some rules of thumb for how we perceive acidities found in the normal range for waters.[28]

Acidic	pH 5–6.7
Neutral	pH 6.7–7.3
Hint of Sweet	pH 7.3–7.8
Alkaline	pH 7.8–10

Resources, Tips, and Tricks

- You'll want a digital scale capable of measuring down to 0.01 g (10 mg). Amazon carries many American Weigh models for about $10.
- My recipe for water is as simple as I could make it and seeks only to make good-tasting water. For many more recipes and resources for reproducing mineral and spring waters with unique taste profiles, see MineralWaters.org, Martin Lersch's work on mineral water at his blog Khymos, or Darcy O'Neill's book *Fix the Pumps*.

---

[28] http://www.finewaters.com/Bottled_Water_Etiquette/Flavor_of_Water/FineWaters_Orientation.asp

- If you can't filter your water or create your own magical mineral water, at least let tap water rest for 20 seconds open to air before using. Most tap water is treated with chlorine, but chlorine escapes rapidly into the air, so it's a good idea to let some of it evaporate off before drinking.
- Particularly hard water can create unsightly pectin gels or even create a buffering effect that could mess with pH. If in doubt, get a cheap total dissolved solids meter (about $15 on Amazon) and check your water. When I checked my tap water, it came out to 350 ppm (yikes!).

Consistently Freeze Crystal-Clear Ice

I obsessed over ice for a long time. I spent over a year building all kinds of contraptions, trying to create perfect cubes and spheres of ice. It began as a fun side project, a way to reproduce the beautiful aesthetics of a top-tier cocktail bar. But as I read books like *The Chemical Physics of Ice*[29] and *Freezing Physics*[30], I became more and more fascinated with the weird science of ice.

I give total credit to Camper English at the Alcademics blog for doing the vast majority of the legwork on learning about ice.[31] His directional freezing method is a great method for making clear ice, especially if you're looking for large sizes or irregular shapes.

What Causes Cloudiness in "Normal" Ice?

Reason #1: Dissolved gases and minerals come out of solution.

Foreign particles dissolve readily in water because water is a powerful polar solvent. But when water freezes, its molecules line up, negative end attached to positive end in a tight structure that leaves no rooms for dissolved particles. As gases are forced out of solution by crystal formation, they are trapped as tiny bubbles that redirect light.

Reason #2: Tiny crystals form within ice's structure and diffract light.

You know how you're supposed to freeze food quickly so smaller ice crystals form? You want the exact opposite effect when making clear ice cubes. This is not the same as dissolved particles coming out of solution due to crystal formation. In this case, the crystals themselves are causing the cloudiness. Here's some science about the phenomenon:

---

[29] by N. H. Fletcher.
[30] by Dirk van Delft.
[31] http://alcademics.com/ice/

> "At its freezing point, water molecules are moving so slowly that they begin to gather in loose, undefined clusters, called seed crystals. As the temperature continues to drop, molecules line up around the seed crystals in increasingly rigid formation until all of the water crystallizes. The longer it takes for crystals to form, the larger they will be."[32]

Reason #3: Water expands when it freezes; expansion causes ice to crack.

Water is most dense at 4°C or 40°F, but it's only slightly less dense at freezing temp, 0°C/32°F. Ice at freezing temperature is 8.3% less dense than liquid water at the same temperature—a substantial difference.

If water cools quickly, a density change can actually occur after the ice has already frozen solid. That's right—molecules within ice continue to shift even in its solid form. Don't believe me? Take a look at this time-lapse video of ice freezing.[33] Notice how as early as 1:00 minute in, air bubbles are trapped in solid ice. But the ice continues to grow significantly well after the entire block turns solid.

A Simple Solution for Clear Ice

In February 2012, a commenter on Camper's blog named Cory Hain posted pictures of the most perfect ice to ever make an appearance on the site. The original photo is reproduced here.

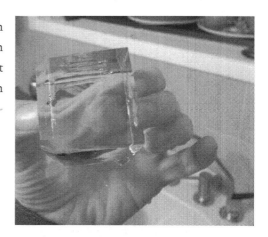

---

[32] Joachim and Schloss, The Science of Good Food (2008), pg. 253.
[33] http://vimeo.com/2816672

I contacted Cory about how he created his ice and here's what he said:

> "The pictures you see come from a dorm room style refrigerator with the partition between the ice box and the main compartment. It creates a 2 zone temperature differential. The upper zone is around 27-31 degrees [Fahrenheit]. Below the glass shelf where the tovolo ice tray sits is about 2 degrees warmer. This creates automatic directional freezing that avoids supercooling."

Cory was convinced that he was able to create clear ice because a high-temperature freeze prevents supercooling, a term used to describe what happens when liquid water stays liquid below 0°C and then suddenly freezes. Supercooling happens in water because water is highly polar and forms crazy crystal structures.

I tested the temperatures Cory used and it works. High-temperature freezing definitely mitigates each of the causes of cloudiness. Because freezing occurs so slowly, minerals and gases are forced to the outsides of the cubes rather than getting trapped inside. Slow freezing also results in larger ice crystals that don't distort light. And finally, expansion happens slowly enough that cracking is avoided.

As for the internet denizens who claim that all it takes to make clear ice is using distilled or boiled water, or thawed and re-frozen water—all I can say is that I've tried it all, and none of those methods work reliably.

Crystal-Clear Ice

some Water
an Ice Tray
a Mini Fridge

Add water to ice cube tray. Turn mini fridge to its warmest setting. Ideally, the freezer compartment will be around 30°F. Place tray and water into freezer compartment. Go do something else for 3-5 days. If you don't have a mini-fridge that can do this, check out the chapter "How to Infuse 200x Faster with Precision Temperature Control" and look under "How to Make Clear Ice, Revisited."

Notes:

- I have to admit that in the months I've been testing this method, I have never been able to make ice quite as clear as Cory's original cube. Doug Shuntich (see below) thinks that maybe because Cory's picture depicts an ice cube that was not completely frozen and that small bubbles would have emerged had he let the ice freeze completely. But from what Doug has told me, achieving truly clear ice would require more precise temperature control than what is possible at home, so I will continue to recommend my/Cory's method for making ice as a good balance between effort and result.

Doug Shuntich on Advanced Topics in Ice

As I was wrapping up work on this book, a commenter on Science Fare named Douglas Shuntich left a detailed and coherent explanation of some of the nuances of ice science. I got in touch with him and found out that Doug had previously worked as a Space Shuttle Launch Systems and Cryogenic Propellant Systems Engineer at NASA. Doug basically agreed with most of what I had written on ice, but he also told me that I was just barely scratching the surface.

Here are his thoughts:

Water in a freezing environment will often supercool to some degree below 32 before it nucleates and begins to freeze. For clearer ice, it's best to have nucleation occur from 29 to 31 degrees. This can be induced with a seed crystal as the water is at the freezing point, or by using warmer water to start. Warmer starting temperatures (such as above 90 degrees) have a steeper temperature decline which causes molecules to be less stable going through two key phases; one at max density (40 degrees) and one at the point of supercooling (32 degrees). This instability seems to act as a catalyst for nucleation at or near the freezing point, resulting in clearer ice crystal formation from the beginning.

Ice releases heat. Keep in mind that nucleation and freezing is exothermic from the first crystal, meaning heat energy at exactly 32 degrees is being given off into the freezer or mini-fridge environment as well as directly into the water that is trying to freeze. When precision temperature control is used to keep the freezing environment above 29 degrees, the exothermic nature of freezing causes the entire process to progress very slowly, resulting in perfectly clear crystal formation.

Timing matters. This is why the temperature control is so critical. Like chocolate, the end structure of a block of ice depends on its crystal structure. Since crystal formation is a stochastic[34] process, simply holding liquid water at a given temperature for a certain amount of time is enough to change the end crystal structure of the ice it forms.

Finally, determining the escape path for air that inevitably gets trapped in the center is a real engineering trick, but can be done using a variety of techniques...

Doug knows a lot more about ice than I've printed here. Read the chapter "Does Hot Water Really Freeze Faster than Cold" at the end of this book for an illustrative case study on how ice freezes. And visit supercoolertechnologies.com in the near future to learn about Doug's game-changing startup.

What do Shaking and Stirring do?

Most bartenders will tell you that a drink with just spirits and liqueurs should be stirred to preserve the silkiness of its texture, while any drink with added syrups or juices must be shaken to properly incorporate all the ingredients. This rule of thumb works well, but here I've broken it down further, as not all drinks are easy to categorize. Which method you choose depends on how you wish to shape a drink's end texture and flavor.

---

[34] It is inherently random and can only be predicted using statistics.

	Stirring	Shaking
Chilling	0°C	-3 to -10°C
Dilution	Less*	More*
Agitation	Low Shear/Simple Mixing	High Shear
Emulsification	No	Yes
Aeration	No	Yes
Volatization	No	Yes

Chilling. Dave Arnold conclusively proved through a series of tests that stirring a drink can chill it down just as cold as that same drink shaken. However, it can take over two minutes to get to the same temperature a shaken drink would reach in 10 seconds. Assuming you get a typical drink, stirred for about 20 to 30 seconds, that drink will likely be sitting at about 0°C. Shaking is a different story altogether. Shaken drinks reach their minimum temperature in about 15 seconds. And that temperature will fall between -3°C and -10°C, depending on the ingredients of the drink. You can see my data on this in the chapter "The Martini: In Pursuit of Perfect Balance."

Dilution*. The vast majority of the chilling that occurs during both stirring and shaking comes from the *heat of fusion*, that is, the amount of energy it takes to melt ice. What does this mean? The colder a drink gets, the more diluted it gets. So, shaken drinks are generally more diluted, as they are typically colder (see above). Why the "*"? Because if you were to stir a drink for two minutes or more, until it was as cold as a shaken drink, it would be slightly more diluted than a shaken drink at the same temperature, since it would have been sitting on the counter exposed to room temperature for a full two minutes while you stirred. But who does that, anyway?

Agitation. Agitation is the mechanical mixing of disparate components. Carefully layer Jameson whiskey over Irish Cream and the two liquids will stay separate indefinitely. Gently agitate the two and they will form a mixture unlikely to separate. Shear describes the amount of force applied to mixing and high shear means that individual bubbles of each liquid are broken into smaller and smaller pieces through kinetic energy. The higher the viscosity a liquid has, the more shear force it requires to fully mix into other ingredients. Therefore, it's a good idea to shake drinks containing thick syrups, for example if you are using Gomme Syrup. Fruit juices are a special case; the pulp and pectin suspended within them can be seen as tiny pockets of high-viscosity liquids that need to be dispersed.

Emulsification/Aeration. Think vinaigrette. Oil and water don't normally mix, but under high shear, they'll break up into smaller droplets and hang out fully mixed with one another, at least for a time. True emulsification happens when the two ingredients that don't like each other are held together by a third party. In the case of vinaigrette, the mucilage in mustard attaches to both oil and vinegar. With cocktails, fats can be emulsified (see "The Flip: Emulsions, With and Without Eggs"), but more often, we're talking about the emulsification of air into a drink. Ambient air will give a cocktail a slightly light feel, reduce flavor release, and in cases where the other ingredients are viscous, form a permanent foam. With non-thickened drinks, the air shaken into a drink will dissipate in about two minutes.

Volatization. When you throw garlic into hot oil, the oil heats the water in the garlic and flavor compounds are expressed into the air. The aroma molecules *volatize.* A single clove of garlic seems to have the power to perfume an entire room. When you shake a cocktail tin as hard as you can, some of the liquid contents inside volatize as well and will float above the glass after you pour the cocktail out.

For the original explanation and some terrific visuals, see Dave Arnold's original post at his blog, Cooking Issues:
http://www.cookingissues.com/2010/09/08/cocktail-science-in-generalpart-2-of-2/

Citrus: How to Maximize Aroma and Preserve Freshness

I believe that if life gives you lemons, you should make lemonade... And try to find somebody whose life has given them vodka, and have a party.

- Ron White, Comedian

It seems weird to think about it now, but just a few years ago, if you ordered a whiskey sour at a bar, the bartender was more likely than not to reach for a bottle of sour mix. It's probably not that he preferred sour mix over fresh juice—back then, most bartenders didn't even realize the two were related.

Today, fresh juice has become the rallying cry for good drinks. I only see sour mix now at cheesy company parties and tucked into the pantries of my bachelor friends, behind other embarrassments like wonder bread and canned ravioli.

So I'm assuming you already know that using fresh juice is important. I won't beat that dead horse. But did you know that limes are almost 1.5 times more sour than lemons? Or that pineapples contain more acid than oranges? How about that it's widely accepted that limes taste better a few hours *after* they're juiced? Let's have a look.

Acid and Sugar Content of Common Citrus Fruits

If you were to take all the juice from an orange and dehydrate it down so only the solids were left, you would be left with a pile of sugar and organic acids. As we discussed earlier, however, acid is only one part of perceiving a food as sour. Just as important is sugar content, as sugar has a strong suppressive effect on acidity. Below is a rough guess at the total acid and sugar contents of the most widely available citrus fruits, based on published scientific work and nutritional databases. [35, 36, 37] More precise numbers are difficult to come by due to the variability within and between varieties of fruit.

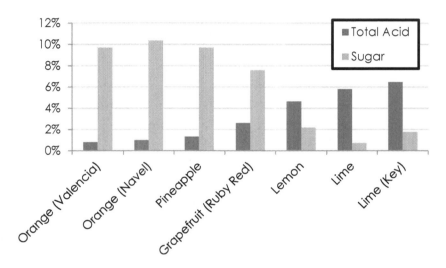

The sugar and acid amounts in the above chart are given in % of total mass of juice. Total sugar accounts for sucrose, fructose, and glucose, corrected for sweetness.

Acid composition also contributes to the flavor and perceived sourness of a juice. Citrus fruits are predominantly citric acid, with some malic and succinic acid thrown in. The latter two are best known for the flavor of apples. Ascorbic acid

[35] Kelebek, *Sugars, organic acids, phenolic compositions and antioxidant activity of Grapefruit (Citrus paradisi) cultivars grown in Turkey (2010)*.

[36] Ladaniya, Citrus Fruit: Biology, Technology, and Evaluation (2008), pp. 129, 136.

[37] Albertini et al., *Changes in Organic Acids and Sugars during Early Stages of Development of Acidic and Acidless Citrus Fruit (2006)*.

also appears in citrus, but contributes less flavor than the other acids. The below charts illustrate the differences between citrus fruits.

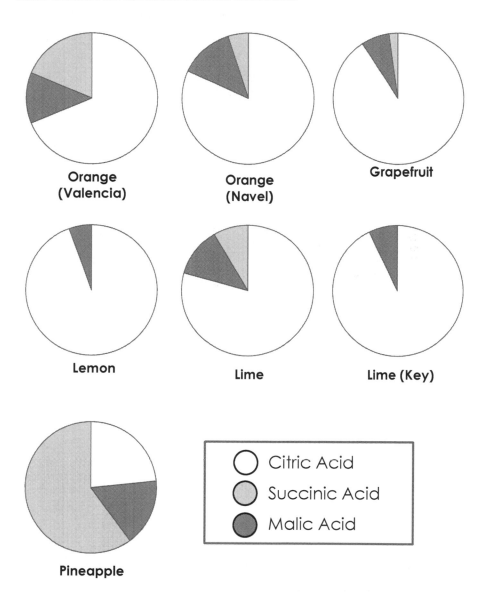

These pie charts represent percent of acid type in total acid content. For more on hacking acid flavors, see the chapter "The Sour: Acid Alternatives to Citrus."

Why does this matter? Well, most importantly, these values help us know how to balance drinks containing sour components. But also notice the similarity between the acid contents of lemons and limes. Both are pretty sour and contain mostly citric acid. So how come they have such distinct flavors? **The answer lies in aroma.**

I spoke with Andrew Cameron of Canvas Club in Woolloongabba (say that 5 times drunk), Australia. Like me, Andrew is very interested in how aroma affects cocktail flavor perception. Here's what he had to say about aroma, amongst other topics.

Andrew Cameron
on Hacking Cocktail Competitions with Science

Photo used with permission of Matthew Williamson Photography[38]

You're a student full time. Tell me about your studies.

I am currently completing my Honours year of my Bachelor of Technology Innovation (Honours) degree at the Queensland University of Technology. I major in microbiology; however my scientific grounding is very broad in the life sciences, covering molecular biology, biochemistry, medical physiology and biotechnology principles as well. I am currently working on measuring success factors in the biopesticide industry and have been out doing work on farms, at the desk and in the

---

[38] https://www.facebook.com/MatthewWilliamsonPhotography

lab. In the past, I've clocked just over a year in Panama and Costa Rica and did some work for Smithsonian Tropical Research Institute in the field of tropical drug discovery.

And you still had time to become a bartender in your spare time?

The way that I see it, bartending is the only field where you get to be a scientist, a historian, a creative and a people person simultaneously, under pressure. For me bartending and cooking are the most applied of sciences, you have the opportunity to do some molecular problem solving multiple times a day, more so if you are working and getting paid to do it, and I love it. Harold McGee, Alton Brown and Heston Blumenthal have a talent for making their way into my life somehow every day, and I am always experimenting.

I have been working hospitality out of passion and a means of scratching that creative itch for more than 6 years now, and have had the privilege of working with some truly great talent, both in the bar and in the kitchen, throughout my career. I am always curious about new innovative methods for generating new experiences for the customer, and transferring skills from the lab to the bar, and the bar back to the lab.

So that's how you ended up at Canvas Club?

Correct. I've been over at Canvas Club in Woolloongabba for just over a year now. We won Australia's Best New Bar in 2011 and we just recently won Australia's Best Cocktail List 2012. We were also nominated for Best Bar Team and Best Cocktail Bar 2012. How I got there? I strongly believe the owners have a talent for finding great cocktail geeks who genuinely care about their product and service. The dream team had me as the science geek who assisted in all cocktail R & D, Glenn Morgan was the Cocktail History and Recipe Almanac, Krystal Hart the Fact-master with the super-senses and Angus Burton was the other mad scientist with a knack for process innovation. Nick Pitts also joined us for a short spell, and was our resident beer nerd for a while.

I first read about your work because we were both doing events for National Science Week. Tell me about what you were doing there with effervescence and aromatics.

I made three drinks—the first one was a "Death in the Afternoon"—a straightforward drink with absinthe and champagne, but one that gave me the chance to explain the science behind effervescence. Next up was my "Stirred not Shaken" drink, which was basically a gin martini where I used liquid nitrogen to chill it to the exact temperature I wanted.

The last one was "An Aromatic Blend". It's basically a breakfast martini. So I actually had the guests drinking those throughout the night, but then toward the end, I asked, "so have you all been enjoying those? Ok, well, we're going to do something interesting with them now." So I had some dry ice and I had made some lemon extract and basically created a lemon fog that I spread around the room. And when I asked them to taste it again, the drink tasted much more of lemon. And of course when I did the same thing, but with an orange tea fog, it tasted more of orange.

I understand you've competed in a number of competitions. Tell me about how science has helped you succeed.

This year I was a finalist for the Angostura Carnival Competition and the 42 Below Masters of Mixology Competition.

For the Angostura competition, I decided to play with the idea of savory and sweet in cocktails, so I actually worked Portugese Bacalhau, a salted cod product, into a drink with Angostura 1824® rum. It was definitely different, but it also ties back to the street food of Trinidad and Tobago, which is where Angostura is made, so there is a local connection there as well. I think the savory element in cocktails is really important. I think if you push the sweetness along one axis, you can push the saltiness along another and you end up with a more complete drink.

At 42 Below, I created a drink I called *The Rutherford* after Ernest Rutherford, who is renowned as the father of nuclear physics. I attempted to recreate a cocktail representation of his famous gold foil experiment that proved that atoms had a nucleus. Before this theory, atoms were thought to be homogenous. Essentially, he fired alpha particles through thin sheets of gold, most went through, but some bounced back because they ran into the gold atoms' nuclei.

To represent the experiment I made some green walnut and quinine alginate pearls with flecks of gold leaf and tossed them into a dry martini made with Feijoa vodka and a pear skin, wormwood and Nelson Chardonnay-infused dry vermouth.

An Aromatic Blend (Aromatized Breakfast Martini)
Courtesy Andrew Cameron, Canvas Club, Woolloongabba, Australia

45 ml Gin (Bombay Sapphire)
20 ml Fresh lemon juice
20 ml Triple Sec
1 barspoon Orange Marmalade (needs to have lots of rind in it)
Lemon Extract
Orange Extract

Combine ingredients, shake, and double-strain.

Serve the drink straight, then spray a spritz of lemon extract into the air over the glass. Taste. Repeat with the orange extract. Compare and contrast.

Notes

- To make the lemon or orange extract, combine lots of zest with high-proof grain alcohol or vodka. Let rest 2 hours up to a day, or blend on low speed in a blender for 5 minutes. Strain. Alternatively, just buy lemon or orange extract from the supermarket. It works quite well.

- Andrew originally used bergamot flavoring for his cocktail. To use bergamot extract instead of orange extract, combine 1 part bergamot essential oil with 100 parts vodka (essential oils are available from health food retailers—search "aromatherapy"). Conveniently, a 100:1 ratio equates to roughly 1 drop essential oil in 1 oz. vodka.

- Read more about concentrated flavors in the chapter "Tinctures, Oils, and Extracts."

- For spritzing, I use 2 oz. blue cobalt atomizer bottles from QEDusa.com, they cost $2.45 per bottle and atomizer combo.

And now a preview of the next section—everything old really is new again:

"**Concentrated Tincture of Lemon Peel**: This combination of lemon peel with the solution of pure lemon acid forms an exact substitute for

Peak Quality: Is Fresh-Squeezed Really Better?

If the taste of fresh citrus juice was just about sweet and sour, it would be easy for food companies to reproduce and market the flavor. Yet every good cook knows that commercial citrus juices are a far cry from the fresh-squeezed version.

The Importance of Oil.

Much of the flavor that we use to differentiate between an orange and a grapefruit is stored in the plant's outer peel, or zest. The fruits' oils are produced by special oil glands that deposit the material into the epidermis. The oil glands also deposit a small amount of these same oils right into the juice vesicles of the fruit, but much more of it ends up on the outer skin.

Hand-squeezed citrus juice is considered to have the best flavor not just because it hasn't been processed, but also because hand-squeezing ruptures the oil sacs in citrus peels and some of that oil makes it into the juice.

Or as Las Vegas-based bartender Kate Gerwin succinctly put it:

ABOVE ALL OTHER THINGS HAND JUICING IS MOST IMPORTANT, THROW AWAY YOUR JUICER NOW AND IF YOU DON'T BELIEVE ME DO YOUR OWN TEST!!! [39]

Aged Juice?

Back during Tales of the Cocktail 2010, well-known technology-inclined bartender/chef Dave Arnold noticed something odd about fresh lime juice. In his eloquently titled blog post, **"Fresh Lime Juice: WTF?"**, he summarized his findings:

---

[39] A comment posted to the drinkology forum mirrored on the Cooking Issues blog resulting from a taste test of different methods for squeezing lime juice. I found it amusing.

At 2PM we separated 1.5 cases of limes into 3 equal piles. I juiced 1 pile in the Sunkist juicer and 1 pile with the hand juicer. We were done by 2:15. We weighed the samples—the machine juicer yielded 26 ounces of juice, the hand juicer 21.5. I then put the juice in covered quart containers and left them out of the fridge.

At 6:15pm I juiced the third pile. We then made limeade by mixing the same amount of each lime juice with measured amounts of water and simple syrup. We served it in a blind tasting at 7pm.

Results:

The overwhelming favorite was the hand-squeezed lime juice that was 4 hours old. The distant second place was 4-hour-old machine-pressed juice. Almost no one chose the fresh hand squeezed juice. Before I revealed what the samples were, I asked those who chose the 4-hour hand-pressed juice to choose a second favorite. They all chose the 4-hour machine juice. I was flabbergasted, and so was the audience.

A handful of fellow geeks replicated Dave's experiment in various experiments and came up with the same or similar results. Most agreed that 4-hour-old juice tasted **less acidic, more "round" or "mellow", with more "nutty" or "madeirized" flavors, or simply that it tastes more "like lime."**

So it appears the majority of the bartending community agrees that aged lime juice does indeed taste better than just-squeezed. But that still leaves the question Dave originally asked unanswered…

WTF?

Researching the how's and why's of lime juice's flavor change proved more challenging than expected—the food science community rarely explores the chemistry of extremely fresh products. Instead, it focuses on optimizing packaging and storage methods to maintain quality over the long term. So I don't have a definitive answer, but we can look at a few possible theories and the evidence behind them.

- **Oxidation.** Harold McGee says that lime juice oxidizes very quickly.[40] I'm not usually one to disagree with Harold, but the evidence for oxidation is weak. Citrus juices contain exceptionally high amounts of the powerful antioxidant ascorbic acid (commonly known as vitamin C). Two different studies[41, 42] showed that even less-acidic orange and grapefruit juices keep over 90% of their ascorbic acid for weeks when refrigerated.
- **Change in pH.** This one's easy. I tested lemon, lime, orange, and grapefruit juices over three weeks. pH does not change significantly.
- **Enzymatic Bittering.** My favorite explanation for the decrease in tartness of aged lime juice. Bartender Stephen Shellenberger explained to me that all citrus fruits contain an enzyme that will produce the bitter compound limonin in the hours immediately after juicing. As we've covered before, a very small amount of bitter flavor can mildly suppress sourness.
- **Changes in volatile aromatic compounds.** This one's tough to measure, but probably contributes a great deal to flavor perception. First off, some volatile aromatics will obviously escape into the air after juicing. But even if you quickly cap freshly squeezed juice, chemical interactions continue to occur. Calling these reactions "oxidation" isn't fair; oxygen plays a role, but so do water and acid. I haven't found any papers that look specifically at the changes in citrus juice in the hours after juicing; measurements usually look at quality after days or weeks of storage. See next section for more details.

The Peak Quality Chart for Citrus Juices

Fruit	Peak Quality (time after squeezing)	Shelf-Life (refrigerated)
Orange Juice	Immediate	2–3 weeks
Grapefruit Juice	1–3 days	2–3 weeks
Lemon Juice	4–10 hours	1–2 months
Lime Juice	4–10 hours	1–2 months

---

[40] http://drinkfactory.blogspot.com/2010/08/harold-mcgee-and-tony-conigliaro.html
[41] Fellers, *Shelf Life and Quality of Freshly Squeezed, Unpasteurized, Polyethylene-Bottled Citrus Juice (2006)*;
[42] Kabasakalis et al., *Ascorbic acid content of commercial fruit juices and its rate of loss upon storage (2000)*.

Notes:

- I tested all of the juices in multiple tastings, using a combination of straight juice, mixed with water, mixed with water and sugar, etc. The tests were not truly scientific and I could have used more tasters, but given my time constraints, I think these tests were at least a good starting point.

- I noticed increased enzymatic bitterness in each juice. In the case of orange juice, it was noticeable and unpleasant after just an hour of storage. In lime and lemon, the bitterness seemed to mellow out some of the acidity at first, but became overpowering after 10 hours. In grapefruit, the bitterness actually made the juice taste more grapefruity and didn't become overpowering for several days.

- Aroma degradation becomes a problem after a day of storage. This is most relevant to grapefruit juice, as it otherwise maintains peak quality for several days. I recommend squeezing the oil from a fresh peel just before service to replace the lost/degraded the aromas.

- I continued to test grapefruit juice for several weeks after I first juiced it. It continued to be useable, if not at peak quality, throughout this time. At two weeks, I noticed a faint off-taste and by three weeks there was noticeable carbonation, which suggested yeast was growing, so I chucked it.

- I didn't test the shelf life of lemon, lime, and orange juices since they're simply not very tasty after being stored for just a few days. According to research,[43] orange juice develops off-flavors after 16–22 days of refrigerated storage, though it will not be dangerous to consume.

- Various sources[44] list a refrigerated shelf life of anywhere from 4 months to 27 months for refrigerated lime juice. My guess is that the high acidity of both lemon and lime juices prevents the growth of microbes enough that any contamination is dependent upon acid-resistant strains present in particular test environments. Regardless, you probably won't want to use either for cocktails after 1 to 2 months in the refrigerator because of the development of off-flavors.

---

[43] Fellers (2006).

[44] For a review, see Hui (ed.), Handbook of Fruits and Fruit Processing (2006), pg. 345.

On fresh fruit:

Citrus fruits keep best stored in the refrigerator, in a humid area if possible. I recommend storing them in a fruit drawer along with a wad of damp paper towels. While under optimal conditions some fruits can last as long as six months, while a good rule of thumb for fruit bought from the supermarket is 3 weeks.[45]

A parting thought:

In some of my research, I found papers that alluded to the fact that off-flavors in fresh juice are actually *caused* by peel oils mixing with the high acidity of citrus juice. I never got around to running my taste tests again, but here's an idea for how to maximize the freshness of citrus juice while preventing those off-flavors.

Fresh Lime Juice

1 Lime

Gently peel the lime and reserve the peels in a shallow bowl of water in the refrigerator. Avoid the white pith as much as possible. Microwave the peeled lime for 10-20 seconds; it should be warm, not hot. Cut the lime in half and juice with a hand juicer into a fresh container. When ready for use, squeeze the lime peels over the juice to release the oils. Use immediately.

---

[45] Ladaniya (2008), pg. 336.

Sugar and Syrup: How Everything Old Becomes New Again

The timeline of the rise and fall (and rise) of cocktails almost exactly mirrors the amount of attention we have paid sugar in modern history. Up until the early 20th century, sugar was a luxury good; our pursuit of it defined trade and exemplified modern science. But by the 20th century, we had learned to bleach, cube, and commoditize sugar, to the point that it fell into the background of perception, the way your little pinky toe is always attached but seldom worth noticing. Today, our awareness of sugar has resurged along with a new but often misplaced awareness of health. Everything from "raw" sugar to miracle berries claim to offer the most health benefits.

In this section, I examine some of the different types of sugar on the market today and offer a few lesser-known tricks for making syrups at home.

Sugar: A Glossary of Terms

Ask any bartender. Sugar is to cocktails what salt and pepper are to a steak. Almost every drink needs sugar in some form and the difference between a good drink and a great one often rests on finding the perfect balance of sweetness to other tastes. Unique sweeteners can be used to up the flavor in a drink, but not all gourmet syrups are worth their price tags. Here is a glossary of sugars to help you make your sweetening choices.

- **Table Sugar.** Refined sucrose. Sugar cane or sugar beets are harvested and pressed. The juice is then evaporated and centrifuged, resulting in crystalline raw sugar. This raw sugar is then repeatedly dissolved in syrup, evaporated, and centrifuged to remove impurities. Finally, the sugar is bleached using chemicals ranging from carbon dioxide to sulfur dioxide (not actual bleach).
- **Glucose or Fructose.** Plain old sucrose is a disaccharide, or two very simple carbohydrates connected together. Those two carbohydrates (in this case, they're called monosaccharides) happen to be glucose and fructose. Glucose

forms a viscous syrup and is 75% as sweet as sucrose. Fructose forms a less viscous syrup and is 175% as sweet as sucrose.

- **Molasses.** When crystallized sugar is separated from cane juice, what remains is molasses. The first processing of molasses typically results in a product with higher sugar content, while the last extraction ("blackstrap" molasses) contains less residual sugar.

- **Brown Sugar.** Refined white sugar with some amount of molasses added back in. Yup, the stuff that was so painstakingly removed in the first place.

- **Raw Sugar.** Sugar that has not been refined as much as white sugar. Essentially, it is white sugar that has been centrifuged, but not bleached. It still contains some molasses so its taste is comparable to that of brown sugar, but with less moisture content. Demerara and Turbinado sugars (see below) are actually types of raw sugars.

- **Organic Sugar.** The term "organic" by itself means relatively little. Most notably, sugarcane used to produce organic sugar must be grown in accordance with USDA organic guidelines. Since USDA organic guidelines don't allow chemical processing, organic sugar cannot be bleached and so will contain a small amount more of its natural molasses.

- **Demerara, Turbinado, and Muscovado Sugars.** Both Demerera and Turbinado sugars are simply raw sugars that have been centrifuged from sugarcane juice but are not further processed. They taste somewhat like brown sugar, but contain less moisture because molasses syrup (and its corresponding water content) has not been added back in. Muscovado sugar is even less refined than Demerera and Turbinado. Muscovado sugar is made by boiling sugar cane syrup and letting it air dry to form a dark, moist sugar that tastes heavily of molasses. Muscovado sugar contains the most naturally-occurring vitamins and minerals of any table sugar.

- **Agave Syrup.** A sweet syrup made from the agave plant—the same plant that's used to produce tequila. These syrups typically contain more fructose than simple syrup, which means they taste sweeter and are less viscous. Depending on the vendor, they may also have some of agave's grassiness.

- **Honey.** Flavor and sweetness of honey depends highly on the source and processing used to produce it, but most honeys contain more fructose than simple syrup. Honey's unique thickness comes from the proteins and other carbohydrates it naturally contains and not from sugar content alone.

Does a Miracle Sugar Replacement Exist?

In a word, no. Sweeteners fall into two broad categories—nutritive and non-nutritive. I've tried many examples and combinations from both categories and have yet to find one that even comes close to the taste of sugar.

Nutritive sweeteners. Sweeteners that contribute significantly to calories. In addition to the sweeteners listed in the previous section, the other basic disaccharides (lactose, maltose, trehalose, and cellobiose) as well as the monosaccharide xylose can be used as sweeteners. Of these, only trehalose tastes like plain sugar and it's difficult to find. Sugar alcohols like sorbitol or mannitol are often used by industrial food producers to create "no sugar added" products, but these products have a cooling effect on the tongue and can cause gastrointestinal distress even when used in moderation.

Non-nutritive sweeteners. Chemicals that taste so much sweeter than sucrose that you can add a nutritionally insignificant amount of them to achieve the same sweetness. I've tested sucralose (Splenda® brand), aspartame, and the new popular sweetener Stevia (Truvia® and NuNaturals™ brands) side-by-side with traditional simple syrup, and the non-nutritive competitors don't come close. Off tastes ranged from "bleach-y" to "bitter" and mouthfeel was completely lacking.

Is it possible to replace sugar? I'm sure that science will find the answer some day, but I'm confident no answer worthy of craft cocktail use exists at the moment. Consider Coca-Cola®. What company in the world is more incentivized to produce a sugar replacement? But even their billion-dollar research abilities have so far only managed to produce Coke Zero, a very good approximation of the full-sugar product, but still clearly different. And that's considering the masking effect of all the acids and bitters already in Coke.

Syrup-Making Tip #1: Turn Off the Heat

As I was browsing around the internet researching cocktails, I stumbled across a chart for the solubility of sucrose in water. In part, it read:

Solubility of sucrose in water at room temperature: 2000 g/L. [46]

After doing some quick math in my head, I made the inevitable, obvious conclusion: **sugar is really soluble.** To make simple syrup, all you need to do is combine sugar with water. No heat required. Yes, it will take a little bit longer, but you get a richer syrup (cooking the sucrose disaccharide breaks it down into smaller, less viscous monosaccharides) and you don't have to fuss over cooling it down before use.

Syrup-Making Tip #2: Trust Mass, Nothing Else.

	Sugar	Water	Concentration
Art of the Bar	1 Cup	1 Cup	
Joy of Mixology	1 Cup	1 Cup	
Modern Mixologist	1 Cup	1 Cup	
Craft of the Cocktail	1 Part	1 Part	
PDT	32 oz	32 fl oz	
Speakeasy	1.5 lbs	2 cups	
Rich Simple (Imbibe!)	2 Parts	1 Part	

Take a look at the graph above. It should be pretty self-explanatory. **Simple syrup recipes vary.** And that's without taking into account the fact that different types of sugar have different densities and that density can change with exposure to moisture.

Another word of caution: syrup volume does wacky stuff. For example, pretend that you do some quick math and decide to add a cup of plain water to 3 cups of 2:1 simple syrup intending to make 4 cups of 1:1 simple syrup. If you did this, you

---

[46] Sucrose, International Chemical Safety Card 1507, Geneva: International Programme on Chemical Safety, November 2003 | via Wikipedia.org

would actually end up with about 3 cups 15 ½ oz. of 1.14:1 simple syrup. Just sayin'—stick to mass.

Easy Simple Syrup
Makes about 1.5 cups (12 oz)

220 g Water
220 g Granulated Sugar

Add sugar to water and sit patiently. Shake at least once, after twenty minutes or so. The syrup should be clear within 30 minutes at room temperature, if not sooner.

The one downside of not first heating a syrup? When you heat a syrup to dissolve the sugar, the heat conveniently kills most of the microbes hanging out in the container. Fewer microbes at the start means slower growth of bad stuff. The next chapter deals with killing microbes and preservation and general.

Preservation: Extend the Shelf Life of Syrups and Vermouths

This is what happens to raspberry syrup after 3 weeks in a 45°F fridge

One of the downsides of setting your mini fridge's freezer to the warmest setting? The rest of it gets pretty warm too. There's a reason why 40°F to 140F is known as "the danger zone."

In this section, we'll talk about preservation techniques for syrups and low-alcohol ingredients like liqueurs and vermouths.

What Causes Spoilage?

Food is considered spoiled when one of two things happens:

1. When a food has become unsafe to eat.
2. When a food's quality has degraded so much that it becomes undesirable.

When dealing with unsafe food, microbes are generally the culprit. I'll address microbes and preservation techniques first. The section on vermouth deals more with quality degradation; also see the chapter on citrus quality.

What is a microbe? "Microbe" is a generic name for any microorganism—a living creature that can only be seen through a microscope. Many different types of microbes exist and can cause harm to people, but I'll focus on the three types most relevant to cocktail mixers: bacteria, mold, and yeasts.

- **Bacteria** are prokaryotes. Common strains include Salmonella and E. coli. Infection is not necessarily visible.
- **Mold** are fungi (like mushrooms). Common types include Aspergillus. Look for fuzzy stuff, dark spots growing, or general opaqueness in a syrup. I've also noticed that simple syrups will develop a slight bitter aftertaste over time, before any visual changes. Chuck the syrup if any bitterness develops.
- **Yeast** are eukaryotic fungi. They are generally not dangerous, but some can cause infection. The tell-tale sign of yeast growing is slight carbonation or acidic flavor. Visible signs of yeast will resemble mold.

Viruses, parasites, and prions (oh my!) can also cause food poisoning, but I think they're less relevant in this context because they are usually spread through infected meat products or poor sanitation in the food supply. I highlight bacteria, molds, and yeasts because they share a common feature: each microbe will be found in every syrup you make—guaranteed.

Yeasts, molds, and bacteria inhabit every corner of the Earth and will infect any food material, even if it is exposed to the ambient air for just a few seconds. While many bacteria and mold (and most yeasts) are not harmful, there are enough harmful strains out there that any signs of contamination should trigger you to throw out the whole batch.

Preserving Syrups

There are no easy formulas for calculating how long a syrup will last. Spoilage depends on ambient conditions as well as how many microbes naturally occur in your neck of the woods. I know that I once stored syrup in a too-warm fridge for just under a week and there was a noticeable off taste. You'll know if syrup has spoiled if it tastes even the slightest bit bitter or if it turns cloudy—a sure sign of mold.

Since the food science community doesn't have a magic equation to estimate shelf-life, it uses the "hurdle" concept: the idea that each type of obstacle to microbial growth can be stacked on top of other obstacles in order to increase defenses against spoilage.

Here are the hurdles you need to know about:

- **Water activity (A_w)**: the percentage, by mass of a material that is water. In foods, sugar and salt combine with carbohydrates to "trap" water and make the resultant A_w less than it would be by mass alone, but this is less of a factor in drinks. Sugar, alcohol, and salt all lower a material's A_w.
- **Temperature**: High temperature kills microbes; low temperature slows their metabolism.
- **Oxygen**: Many microbes require oxygen to fuel their nastiness. Removing or replacing oxygen usually reduces microbe activity level.
- **Acidity**: Most microbes (see previous page) can only survive in an ideal pH range. Rule of thumb: lower is better.
- **Chemical preservatives**: Basically, everything else. Ethanol is a chemical preservative because it discourages microbial growth more than its effect on A_w alone.

Bartenders will often add a spoonful of vodka to simple syrups as a preservative. As discussed above, alcohol reduces water activity. But it also acts as a powerful anti-microbial agent, which makes it a chemical preservative (alcohol hand sanitizer, anyone?). That makes ethanol a two-hurdle additive. What sort of effect does this have on shelf-life? Luckily for us, Camper English took the time to measure how much of an effect this trick really has:

> I made up four syrups and decided to wait to see how long it was until they spoiled. For each ratio, I added a tablespoon of vodka, as this is another method of making syrup last longer before spoiling.
>
> 1:1 simple syrup
> 1:1 simple syrup plus one tablespoon vodka
> 2:1 rich simple syrup
> 2:1 rich simple syrup plus one tablespoon vodka

Then I put them all in the refrigerator and waited. Eventually, the syrup would become cloudy then that cloudiness would start to mold. I stopped the experiment when the cloudiness appeared.

Results:

1:1 simple syrup lasted One Month

1:1 simple syrup plus one tablespoon vodka lasted Three Months

2:1 rich simple syrup lasted Six Months

2:1 rich simple syrup plus one tablespoon vodka lasted more than six months[47]

I prefer 1:1 simple syrup because it's easier to pour and measure. And three months is a pretty good lifespan. But what if you're making a special syrup that you'd like to keep for a longer period of time?

Safe Chemical Preservatives?

Benzoic acid is an antimycotic agent that inhibits the growth of yeast, mold, and bacteria. It is generally recognized as safe (GRAS) in the United States up to a concentration of 0.1%, though most countries allow concentrations of 0.15%-0.25%. Any benzoic acid works to inhibit the microbes; sodium benzoate is used because it is highly soluble in both water and alcohol.

Sorbic acid works much the same way and can also be used at 0.1% in syrups. Once again, the potassium is only there to help diluition. Potassium sorbate and sodium benzoate work together; when used together, they have a very strong synergistic effect.

---

[47] Original post: http://www.alcademics.com/2009/08/simple-syrup-its-good-to-be-rich.html

Shelf-Stable-ish Simple Syrup Concentrate
Makes enough to preserve 10 cups of 1:1 simple syrup

95.5g Water
Sugar
2.25g Potassium Sorbate
2.25g Sodium Benzoate

Just like my recipe for tap water, it's easier to make a concentrate of the minerals, then combine with syrup. Mix the potassium sorbate and sodium benzoate with 95.5g of water. This will give you a concentrate with 2.25% by mass of each mineral.

Measure out 10g of the concentrate and add to 1 cup (224 g) of 1:1 simple syrup. Add 10g of sugar and allow to dissolve. At this point, you should have just over a cup of simple syrup, with a total mass of 244 g. The concentrations of each preservative will be 2.25g/244g=0.092%, or just under 0.1% of total mass.

Notes:

- Both sodium and potassium are electrolytes essential to bodily function. Both are flavorless and odorless. There has been some anecdotal evidence that sodium benzoate produces an allergic reaction, but clinical tests were only able to produce symptoms when subjects ate more than 8 grams of the stuff. Potassium sorbate has never been shown to be harmful in any way and is generally considered one of the safest food preservatives known.

- This concentrate can be added to any syrup. Most fruits are acidic, and many spices have antimicrobial properties, so syrups made from those ingredients will probably last even longer than simple syrup.

- Both potassium sorbate and sodium benzoate are available through beer homebrewing supply stores. Amazon carries each for under $10 an ounce and an ounce is enough to preserve over 100 cups of simple syrup.

Preserving Wines and Vermouths

A vermouth will usually not "spoil" the way a syrup does. The sugar, alcohol and some of the herbs used in vermouth act as hurdles to microbial growth. That's not to say microbial spoilage doesn't happen. Even vermouth will turn into vinegar given enough time and acetic acid bacteria. But vermouth, like any good wine, will rapidly lose its quality as soon as it is opened. The culprit? Oxygen.

Evil Oxygen

Oxygen deteriorates wine in two ways. When you open a bottle of vermouth, you expose it to outside oxygen for the first time since it was bottled. Pour out a small amount of the wine and the space it occupied fills with oxygen-rich air. This oxygen reacts both with esters, terpenes, and other volatile aromatic compounds responsible for light, fresh, fruity, and floral flavors found in wine.[48]

Compounds that lose electrons and bind with oxygen are called reducing agents. These include phenolics, which are responsible for some of the astringency and color of red wine. That means that red wines are more able to weather oxidation without harmful effects (in fact, some oxidation is usually considered a good thing in red wines). But it also means that vermouths (which are almost always made with white wine) are particularly vulnerable to oxidation.

The second way oxygen does damage? It's pretty obvious, actually. Give volatile aromatics a little room and they'll... volatize. That's it. You probably won't notice a difference after the first few half-ounce pours, but when you've opened that bottle of Dolin Dry a half dozen times, you'll be able to taste (smell?) a significant difference.

A Simple Solution

I was turned on to this technique by Rob Trzepacz (pronounced tray-pahz), who wrote in to the Cooking Issues Radio Show. Rob splits new bottles of vermouth into mini bottles and purges the headspace with a can of PrivatE PreservE™ Wine Preserver.[49] PrivatE PreservE uses a blend of gases, including argon, an inert gas

---

[48] Jackson, Wine Science Principles and Applications (2008), pg. 503; originally Roussis et al., *Inhibition of the decline of volatile esters and terpenols during oxidative storage of Muscat-white and Xinomavro-red wine by caffeic acid and N-acetyl-cysteine (2005).*
[49] oH loOk I aM So LeeT.

that's heavier than air, which means that it sinks down to the surface of the liquid, purging oxygen from the bottle. In Rob's words:

I found that Fever Tree Tonic Water and Ginger Ale are bottled in 200 mL glass bottles that accept regular caps and that 187 mL champagne splits also take standard bottle caps. It is convenient that you can pack a fifth into 4 small bottles. So after a few Gin and Tonic's, Horses Neck's and French 75's I collected enough bottles to rebottle my collection. A local wine shop had canned wine preserver gas (Argon) that I used to purge the head space.

I experimented with different dispensing techniques to get an effective blanket using a bottle filled with water and a match. One drawback to canned gas is that the pressure is high at first then dissipates as you use it. I found 7 quick sprays towards the side of the bottle did the trick and checked the blanket by putting a lit match in the opening just below the crown. If the match went out immediately I reasoned there was no oxygen. I then used the same technique on the fortified wines. When I noticed a different pressure flow out of the can I checked with the water blank.

The attached (poor quality cell phone) photo shows the results.

I use a slightly modified version of Rob's technique. I use 12-oz. sized used Diet Coke bottles because I always have a steady supply of these on hand and because they can easily be recapped after opening.

A view of my "cocktail accessories" cabinet. In this picture, dry vermouth is bottled in Sprite bottles, and Dubonnet Rouge is in Diet Coke bottles.

HARDWARE

Choose and Buy Hard-to-Find Glassware

Although alcohol has been enjoyed since 8000 B.C. and distilled spirits since around the 14th and 15th centuries A.D., modern glassware did not take root until around the 1850s.[50] Before then, wine and spirits were likely to be found served in silver, wooden, leather, or ceramic vessels of varying sizes and shapes.[51]

How did cocktails change glassware in the United States?

Dean Six on the Origins of Cocktail Glassware

Dean Six is the Executive Director of the Museum of American Glass in West Virginia. He also holds the title of "Crystal Expert" at Replacements Ltd., the world's largest retailer of china, crystal, and glassware.

The cocktail in its original form (spirit, sugar, bitters) has existed since the beginning of the 19th century; the first cocktail book was released in 1862. In what types of vessels would these drinks most likely have been served?

The earliest printed and illustrated glass catalogs date to the early 1870s and are nearly concurrent with the release of the first cocktail book. It is in those catalogs that we find the earliest documentation of which glasses were called what. The captions of catalog pages are valid indications of a glass's intended use.

Most early stemware served one of three purposes. Every pattern illustrated in an early *M'Kee & Brothers of Pittsburgh* catalog included a wine, champagne, and goblet (water) glass. Each was identical in form and differed only in size. Note that the wineglasses of the 19th century were generally only 2 oz. in capacity. One pattern, the "Eugenie" also includes a cordial: a stemmed glass identical in form to the other three, but smaller yet in size.

---

[50] http://www.westernstatesglass.com/index.php/glass-history-menu
[51] http://www.chiff.com/a/wine-glass-history.htm

A slightly more recent catalog from *Bakewell, Pears & Co.*, is titled "Bar Tumblers" and shows over 50 designs. With very few exceptions, these are all low, wide flat tumblers. One is a "jigger"; a slightly larger one is a "bitters" tumbler, and several are "1/3 pint" (5.3 oz) or "1/2 pint" (8 oz) tumblers. Some are labeled as simply "bar" tumblers. The majority of these tumblers are straight sided, wide, and sit flat, without a stem.

Other than a significant number of goblets made for water by a wide variety of manufacturers and a handful of glasses specific to ale and beer, the predominant glassware of the 19th century into the early 20th were wine and champagne stemware and tumblers.

The original cocktail became known as the old-fashioned cocktail, and later simply as an "old-fashioned." It's probably no coincidence that the small glass in which this drink is served is also called an old-fashioned. Why do you think this glass was designed or paired with its eponymous beverage?

Mirroring the fashion of the time, it would seem to follow logic that if one were to serve a drink and call it an "old-fashioned" then the most likely vessel to hold such a libation would sport the same name. As the evidence I've reviewed shows, the vast majority of barware in the mid-19th century was a flat tumbler. If you were to look at these antique glassware catalogs, you would see that today's "old-fashioned" glass is little changed from the tumblers that were in fashion 150 years ago.

Most modern bartenders assert that today's glassware is larger than the glassware that was available when many classic cocktails were created (pre-1930s). Is this assertion actually true, and if so, do you have any idea as to why this happened?

Why did drinks get larger? Because we are Americans and we like everything to be bigger. Just look at the portions of food we now serve. In my youth a soda was a 6-7 ounce glass bottle of cola. Today sodas start at 12 ounces and grow from there. Wine was served in the mid-19th century in a two ounce glass. Today's wine glass start at 5 oz. and fish-bowl-like glasses called a "balloon" glasses have even come into fashion. I suggest that we, as a culture, simply have embraced the idea of grandness in most things. Like our country, our lives and our measures strive to be huge, expansive, and boundless.

Wine experts recommend different glasses for different wines. The same is true of scotch connoisseurs. These glasses are designed to accentuate the aromatic qualities of the liquid inside. Can you provide insight into who (or what company) first pioneered this science?

I wonder if these glasses were the result of science or marketing? I suggest it was marketing and the science to support or further expand the glass offerings came much later.

In Victorian times the emerging middle class found a celebration of tableware a good expression of their new-found prosperity. 19th century tables became an overpopulated space full of specialty items for each course or delicacy. Forks were specialized for fish, asparagus, sardines and much more. Other serving piece became as diverse, specific and elaborate. A fashionable hostess could dazzle guests with her endless tableware. While silver and flatware led the proliferation, china and glass specialization also grew.

For glass, the late 1910s prohibition movement slowed the need for a variety of stems and other drinking vessels. The glass industry (tableware and bottles specifically) was stung by years of lost business due to prohibition. When repeal came in 1933 the variety of glass drinking forms exploded. With the market reset and competitors and a relatively level playing field, I suggest that it was fashion, more than science, that moved consumer to forget the old standards of glassware and embrace new forms.

The first mention I know of where a wine guru participated in the shaping of stemware specifically designated for certain wines was Julian Street (a prominent early wine expert) and his line, that had his signature on each piece, from Morgantown Glass.

Within a few years of repeal the larger table ware manufacturers were introducing extensive drinkware lines.

Fostoria Glass of Moundsville WV introduced a significant number of lines immediately following repeal. Some of these were early market offering of diversity. Blank 6011 was introduced in 1934. It had a goblet, claret, wine, sherry, cocktail, crème de menthe a.k.a. Rhine wine, cordial, brandy, saucer champagne, low sherbet, footed whiskey, oyster cocktail, footed juice, footed tumbler and footed iced tea—a vessel for most things one could imagine wishing to drink! This seems typical of the profusion of patterns and forms offered in the years after repeal and before WWII slowed glass production due to labor and raw material restrictions.

Choosing Glassware

Approach #1: bespoke fit. As Dean explains above, early glasses were designed simply to fit the drinks they were meant to contain. That approach remains valid today. Most cocktails have an alcohol content somewhere between 10 and 20%, which means that a one-alcoholic-drink equivalent cocktail should be between 3 and 6 fluid ounces. Allowing room for ice and spillage, martini and single old-fashioned glasses should hold 4 to 5 ounces, while highball and collins glasses should hold between 8 and 10 oz.

Approach #2: listen to the wine people. I couldn't find any scientific papers or textbooks dealing with glassware's effect on aroma, but pour two measures of the same wine—one into a shot glass and the other into a wine bowl—and observe the difference in aroma profiles. The extra headspace above the liquid allows aromas to concentrate and be perceived more intensely. There's no reason not to apply the same concept to cocktails, particularly aromatized or hyperdiluted drinks. See the chapter "The Manhattan and Hyperdilution" for examples.

Buying Glassware

After searching for some time, I've discovered that finding the right traditional glassware for cocktails can be a real pain in the butt. These small glasses can be hard to find because major manufacturers lack the incentives to produce and market them en masse. Cocktail enthusiasts scour thrift stores, garage sales, and eBay to find the perfect glass. Here are the best sites I've found to get the right glasses online.

- Industry-leader Libbey brand glasses, available in increments from 4 to 24. average cost: $6/glass (for a 4-pack) free shipping for orders over $50. http://www.awesomedrinks.com/
- On Amazon, the only decent glasses I found that could be shipped in small amounts are the Schott Zwiesel series. Available in packs of 6. They offer a highball, an 11 oz. double old-fashioned, and a 5.1-oz. single old-fashioned. average cost: $7/glass (free shipping with Amazon Prime)
- The Boston Shaker sells brand new 5.5 oz. Libbey coupes for $7.50/glass + shipping
- Fishs Eddy sells high-quality highball, rocks, coupe and martini glasses for $4/glass + shipping. My current favorite supplier. Thanks to blog commenter Chris Harrison for the tip.
- Replacements, LTD specializes in replacing broken glassware from sets. They have a huge selection of classic glassware. The site is hard to search, but you can find some real gems. Try searching for "tall sherbet" and then run through some of the filters on the left side to find the glass you want. Glasses start at $2 and can get expensive for rare finds.

How to Properly Chill a Glass—and Does it Matter?

Actually, it makes more of a difference than I expected. Glass has a pretty low thermal diffusivity, which basically means that whatever temperature it starts off at, it tends to maintain for longer than, say, metal. For cocktails, this means that while the temperature of your glass won't drastically change the temperature of the drink, it will affect how the temperature changes over time.

Fellow cocktail geek Fred Yarm did some tests of glassware differences and showed that it makes a big difference whether you use a chilled glass or not. Warm glasses quickly drive a drink's temperature above freezing. The thicker the glass, the warmer the drink gets.

Not making sense? Just look at the pretty picture.

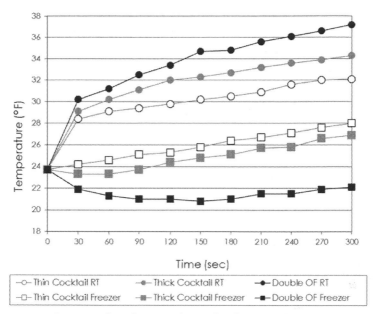

Courtesy of Fred Yarm, the Cocktail ~~Virgin~~ Slut Blog

- In the graph, RT stands for "room temperature" and Double OF refers to the Double Old Fashioned glass Fred used for his tests.
- The glassware all started out at freezer temperature, around 4°F. The cocktails started out at 24°F after being shaken with ice.

Fred also noted that simply swirling ice around a glass with some water doesn't cut it. Fred found that it takes a full 5 minutes to chill glasses to their coldest point (about 40°F). Glasses straight from the freezer start closer to 4°F and can keep drinks cool for much longer. Notice how in the above graph, the drinks served in thick glasses that had been chilled in the freezer actually get *colder* before they start warming up again.

Fred goes into *much* greater detail in a series of three posts at Cocktail ~~Virgin~~ Slut. Look under the category label "barware."

Next, we'll look at how to change the appearance of what goes *in* the glass.

For Every Particle, a Filter

The typical recipe for an infused liquor or syrup always lists as a final step "strain through three layers of cheesecloth." For every infusion recipe I've listed in this book, there were at least ten I left out—usually because it was impossible to filter out the solids from the liquids. Here are a few specific tips and tricks I've used and your best bets for when to apply them. Oh, and here's a spoiler: I never use cheesecloth anymore.

First, let's get one thing straight: there is no such thing as filtration without flavor removal. Every time you filter a liquid, it loses some of its taste and aroma. As a result, whether or not to filter a liquid always becomes a balancing act, weighing flavor against appearance or texture.

I spoke with Sorell Massenburg, a researcher who studies filtration to get the details about what filtration is and some of the specific filtration problems that have plagued my cocktail experiments. Our conversation is below.

Sorell Massenburg Explains the Types of Filtration

Sorell studies how the shapes and sizes of water filter pores affect the way particles clog at Harvard University.

When most people think filtration, they think "water filter". Is that what you study?

Sort of. Most charcoal water filters primarily use adsorption to filter out particulate matter. That is, the charcoal actually reacts with impurities in water and holds onto them. This is a chemical reaction. My research looks at physical filters. Physical filters have tiny pores that separate impurities from water. They're simple, really. If the impurities are larger than the pores, they won't pass through.

It must not be that simple! For example, when I brew coffee, sometimes the water runs straight through the grinds, but sometimes it seems to take forever. What's going on?

When the coffee gets stuck in the filter, then you've probably got clogging going on. That's what I study. When the water can run through freely, that type of filtration is called jamming.

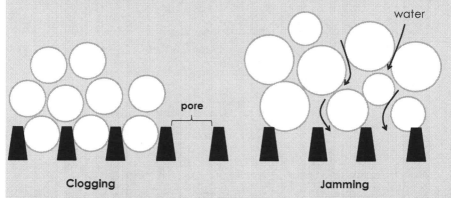

It depends on the relationship between particle size and pore size. If the particles are sufficiently large, they will be stopped by the pores, but they won't clog them up and water will be able to travel through the small spaces between particles. Coffee's actually a great example in that the flow of water depends not only on the pore size of the coffee filter, but also on how the coffee grounds themselves get packed up. The grounds end up forming their own sort of filter in addition to the paper filter. This is known in my field as a "filter cake".

Sounds delicious. Some of the most challenging materials I've tried to filter are plant matter. Is this because plant matter contains long-chain pectins and other carbohydrates?

Well, in a way, you're simply dealing with a filter cake again, only this time instead of chunks and spheres, you end up with a mesh of long interweaving molecules, like a woven basket. In my research, I usually deal with absolute pore size—that is, every one of the pores in the filters I use will be 10, or 20, or however many microns in radius. But it's actually more common in real life to deal with nominal or equivalent pore size. Cheesecloth is a good example. The more layers of cheesecloth you use, the smaller the nominal pore size. It's similar with plant matter. The more strands of carbohydrates floating around, the smaller the nominal pore size. And with many plants, that pore size gets really small really fast.

My Physical Filter Recommendations

The rest of this section is ordered by filtration technique, organized from coarse to fine filtration.

The fine-mesh strainer: ~500 microns. A must have for every kitchen. Basically, nothing more than your standard chinois. I use the OXO Good Grips 8" model because it gives extra surface area for clogging and is very durable. Two ways to use this: for normal application, simply pour through. For fibrous materials, use a ladle to work the liquid around the strainer to make use of more of the surface areas.

The basic cheesecloth replacement: ~100-250 microns. I hate cheesecloths. Also, they respond poorly to pressure. You see, the more layers of cheesecloth you use, the smaller the equivalent pore size in microns. However, the absolute pore size never changes. This means you can end up with very inconsistent results, or easily tear the cheesecloth. Oh, and have you ever tried forming three layers of awkwardly shaped cloth into a well-sealed bag?

Why not just buy a bag? Superbags have become popular recently in the culinary world, but I just can't stomach the $40 price tag. Instead, I love Vermont Fiddle Heads' nut milk bags.[52] They cost only $8 a piece, are durable, and work way better than cheesecloth. Use these bags as a secondary straining step, after the fine mesh strainer.

Crazy Hackery Involved: ~1-10 Microns. Time to break out the coffee filters. But not your typical coffee filters—those only get down to about 15 microns, at best. Worse, they clog easily and rely on slow, slow gravity to work. Here's a different approach:

I stumbled on this brilliant technique while researching home coffee roasting. Coffee hacker Scott Marquardt buys a polyester filter bag, cuts rounds out of it, and hacks it to fit into an AeroPress® coffee maker.

---

[52] http://www.vt-fiddle.com/rawfood/nut_milk_bags_sprouting_bags.php

The 1-micron filter bag

To make the slightly thicker polyester fit into an AeroPress®, Scott files down parts of the AeroPress® to make it fit. I think this is more trouble than it's worth, so I simply cut the polyester round slightly smaller than the paper filter and used the two in conjunction.

Cut the polyester filter slightly smaller than your standard coffee filter.

Use this technique for extremely clear infusions. Keep in mind, however, that the filter clogs easily. Hard particles, such as ground up spices and dried herbs work best. In my experience, fibrous materials were a huge pain and I could only filter out about half an ounce before I had to rinse off the filter. It's ok to use the filter as many times as you like, or until the residual flavors trapped become noticeable.

Note:
- For many more pictures, details, science, and links for purchasing what you'll need, see Scott's original post at: http://marquardts.org/Coffee/invertedaeropressingforbettercoffee.html.

How to Filter Anything

Traditionally, fruit and vegetable infusions are made by steeping the product in high proof alcohol and relying on diffusion and osmosis to slowly draw out desirable flavors. This works, but it takes an incredibly long time, on the order of weeks. If you were to apply shear force, the infusion would occur much more quickly, but pectins and starches would quickly cloud the drink and be very difficult to remove. Below are the specific techniques I've tried that worked for particular ingredients.

Liquor infusions

- **Coconut and other fatty stuff.** One of the hardest ingredients to deal with due to its high fat content. Filter through multiple stages of physical filters. Freeze as cold as possible to solidify the fat and prevent clogging. Google "fat-washing." Other ingredients this technique applies to: **butter, bacon,** and **cocoa.**
- **Porous fruits (strawberries, raspberries, watermelon).** Slice these fruits thin if possible and use the sous vide method.
- **Heat-sensitive fruits.** If you detect off flavors from the sous vide method, blend the fruit with the liquor on the lowest speed for five minutes, leave in the freezer overnight or until the solid matter settles on the bottom of the bottle. Siphon the clear liquid on top out with an aquarium hose or pour carefully. This method is known as racking.
- **Teas and herbs.** Use hot water or the sous-vide method. I haven't tried sous-vide with dred herbs, but others have said it works well. Use the multi-step filtration system, with the AeroPress® as the final step.
- **Hard spices.** Blend spirits and spices on low in a blender for 5 minutes. Use the multi-step filtration system, with the AeroPress® as the final step.

Syrups

- **Spices.** Infuse the spices into water first, preferably hot or sous-vide. Filter the spices using physical multi-step filtration, then add sugar as if you were making a simple syrup.
- **Fruits and vegetables.** Slice the ingredient thin, toss is into a zip-top bag with sugar, and let sit at room temperature, 4 to 8 hours. Osmotic pressure draws the flavors out of the food with minimal cell destruction. This method should work in conjunction with sous vide, but I haven't tested it.
- You can also use any of the juicing techniques described below and add sugar afterward.

Juices

- **Cryo-juicing.** I first found this idea via Aki and Alex of Ideas in Food. Basically, you can freeze, thaw, and refreeze ingredients to cause ice crystals to destroy cell walls and allow juice to leak out. See my recipe for "Cryo-Juiced Cucumber" in the "Drinks to Convert Cocktail Novices" chapter for an example.
- **Gelatin/Agar filtration.** Use a normal juicing machine or tool. Combine the resulting juice with agar agar or gelatin and allow to set. For the gelatin method, freeze overnight, then let thaw in the refrigerator for two days, suspended over a fine mesh strainer. For the agar method, freeze overnight, then allow to thaw at room temperature in a strainer bag; massage the bag to accelerate release of fluids. Both methods will release liquid through a phenomenon known as syneresis while the gelling agent holds on to all solid particles. This is my least favorite method because it strips away a lot of flavor and because it's slow and takes effort. The benefit is that it will produce an extremely clear product.

Dushan Zaric on Infusion

See more of Dushan's thoughts in the chapter "How to Properly Balance a Drink: Two Approaches."

You make a lot of your own syrups. Have you ever experimented with proper infusion times? Do you have any tips to share from your experiences?

That's a great question by the way. Most people don't know how to infuse. I've worked out two ways.

When I infuse vodka I infuse it very simply by adding dry or freeze-dried botanicals, fruits, or herbs into the vodka. I then strain through cheesecloth. Vodka is a cold infusion for me, and I do it—depending on the ingredients—anywhere from a day to about a week. No more than a week.

If I'm infusing other things like gin with lavender, or infusing vermouth, I usually do a hot infusion, which means I do it bottle by bottle. I take out eight ounces from the bottle and then I heat those eight ounces up in an espresso machine. I am very aware that I will lose some of the alcoholic content through the process of heating it, but what I am gaining is a much faster infusion time. Essentially, I'm creating an essence. Once the liquid is hot, I add the botanicals, just like how I would make a tea. I put the botanicals in a tea bag, add it to the hot water, and then let it cool to room temperature. Then I remove the botanicals and I strain that right back into the bottle I poured it out from.

But just how much of a difference does hot versus cold infusion make? Let's take a look.

How to Infuse 200x Faster with Precision Temperature Control

When most people talk about modern gastronomy, they think of the technology of "sous-vide," a French term meaning "under vacuum." For sous-vide cooking, the chef vacuum seals food in a plastic bag and heats it in a water bath set to a precise temperature. The technique ensures perfect doneness and requires very little active effort.

Professional sous-vide setups can run into the thousands of dollars. Home counter-top versions run at least $300 to $400. The high cost is usually due to costly heating elements, and the need to protect all the components from moisture (water baths get humid).

There are plenty of cocktail techniques that use vacuum technology, but I'm going to focus on the temperature control part. The basics of temperature control are relatively cheap. You will need a proportional-integrative-derivative (PID) controller that runs about $35, as well as a few other electrical components that will end up costing no more than $100. I've built four different versions of an at-home sous vide setup.

Unfortunately one short-circuited itself and died. Another one melted and fell into a pot of water (talk about moisture problems). I'm hoping you can learn from my mistakes. I used designs posted by Scott Heimendinger of <u>Seattle Food Geek</u> mashed–up with instructions from Lisa and Abe of the blog <u>Q and Abe</u>. These three folks have each served as major inspirations to me in my exploits into food hackery because they have all turned their hobbies into successful business ventures—Scott now works for Modernist Cuisine and Lisa and Abe have started a promising new product that you can read about below.

Lisa Qiu and Abe Fetterman on DIY Cooking

Lisa and Abe published influential designs for a "$50 DIY sous vide immersion heater/circulator" and a "$70 DIY sous vide universal controller" on their blog Q and Abe. Their latest project, the Nomiku, is making precision temperature control accessible to the home cook.

Your first post was from late 2010, in which you built your first DIY low-temperature cooker. Fast forward two years, you've built a DIY-temp controller kit, taught at hackerspaces, and are currently involved in the Nomiku. What made you focus so much time and energy on this project?

The main reasons we kept working on the Ember Kit/Nomiku are that we were really excited about the food we were cooking, and we loved helping other people to cook the same way without paying through the nose. We were so passionate about the food, but people didn't get what we were talking about because low temperature cooking had been so inaccessible. We wanted to show people it didn't have to be hard. And we really had a fun time meeting hackers and talking to chefs.

You've made a number of updates to your first design. Can you talk about the design process?

Although I [Abe] have a physics background, I had never done circuit layout or design. So I was learning a lot, and the early boards were functional but not easy to assemble. The main design changes have been from watching people build the kit and trying to make each step easier and more intuitive. There haven't been any exciting failures during development, fortunately. Safety is always most important when mixing high voltages and water.

My roommates once came home to find a slow-cooker rigged up to what looked like a countdown timer. "Bomb chicken" was born. How do you get less tech-minded friends to take a leap of faith and start reading wire diagrams to make dinner?

I think the people who built the Ember Kit were all pretty tech-minded. From the start we've tried to make the product *usable* by anyone, but assembly is definitely a task for experts.

What's the most delicious thing you ever made with technology?

We've had a lot of experiments, but I have to say low temperature salmon is as good as any dish you will get anywhere.

What's the most crazy/weird/disastrous dish you ever made?

We once tried to make an olive oil cake in a ziploc bag with the Ember Kit. It was a valiant effort, but in the end it was just what you'd expect: a pile of mush.

What's your favorite cocktail?

I <3 Negroni.

Make Your Own Universal Temperature Controller

There isn't room here to lay out the instructions step-by-step, so instead I'll explain in plain English how all the major components work. See the end of this section for links to wiring diagrams and detailed builds.

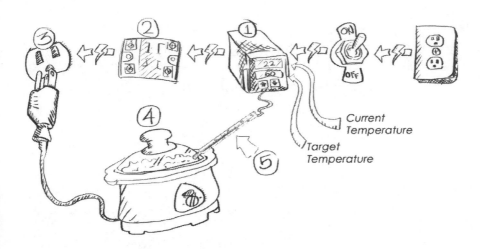

Current Temperature

Target Temperature

(1) **PID Controller**. PID stands for proportional-integrative-derivative. Have you ever started swerving on an icy road and it seemed like no matter how you turned the wheel, you couldn't get the car straight again? In systems engineering terms, you were not providing the system with the right amount of input to correct the error.

Think about temperature like a system. In a normal oven, the heating element is set to turn on whenever the temperature gets too low and shuts off once it returns to the target temperature. But ovens don't account for carryover heat, so they constantly give the system the wrong amount of input. Your typical oven swerves around the temperature it's set to like a compact car in an ice storm.

A PID controller measures the temperature using three different approaches—hence the proportional, integrative, and derivative components to the name. I won't bore you with the details here; just know that the bulk of the device is devoted to circuitry that executes complex equations. As the operator, you simply need to know how to program and connect the device to other components.

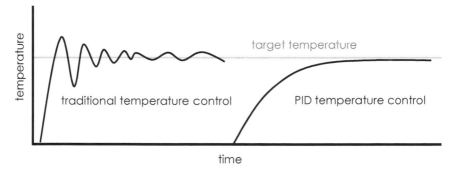

The PID controller sends rapid on and off signals to the heating element it controls. But the controller itself can only put out a very small amount of electricity— nowhere near enough to power anything. The **(2) solid state relay (SSR)** provides the resilience to switch on and off larger amounts of current. In traditional sous vide builds, the SSR connects directly to a heating element. For a universal controller, we'll instead wire it to an **(3) outlet** and plug our **(4) heating element** into that.

Finally, the **(5) temperature probe** should go into the compartment where the temperature is to be controlled. In the case of a water bath for sous vide, that would be the water. For a mini-fridge, the probe would go either on the top shelf or in the freezer compartment, wherever you're trying to make clear ice.

Configuration instructions:

The PID controller does not come configured properly out of the box! I don't know why more DIY guides don't harp on this, but luckily Lisa and Abe provided solid instructions. These specific configuration instructions work for the JLD612 PID controller, though the parameters should work for any controller. The menu steps will simply be different.

> "In our formulas we varied parameters all over the place until we got something that converges as fast as possible in most situations (i.e. small pots, big pots, different heaters, covered, uncovered, etc.). However, this diagram simulates a middle-of-the-road model of a semi-covered pot 30 cm in diameter, with 20 cm of water and a 1000 W heater for heating and evaporative cooling. You can see in the figure the original temperature curve (green), after auto-tuning (red), and with our new PID parameters.

The optimized parameters: P: 0.2%; I: 2000 sec; D: 0 sec.

Press SET; enter code "0036"; press SET; press up or down to P; enter 00.2; press SET; press up to I; enter 1999; press SET; press up to d; press SET; enter 000; press SET. Press up or down to End; press SET. The parameters will remain set even after your controller is unplugged."[53]

Other Stuff You'll Need:
- I really recommend having some sort of Tupperware to house all the components. It makes it that much easier to whip the device out when you need it and store it when you don't.
- Electrical tape, a few feet of wire, and an extension cord
- Some spade or ring terminals for connecting wires to the various components. I prefer spade terminals over ring terminals because they are easier to use. They come in different sizes, so make sure to get one that fits the components. Google how to crimp these guys; it's not as intuitive as it looks.
- Some nice to haves: A crimping tool for stripping wires and crimping terminals, a Dremel to cut holes in Tupperware, scissors, a hot glue gun to hold components steady in your container.
- See any of the links under detailed instructions, below, for information on buying the materials you'll need.

Tips and Tricks
- Think about the order in which the components will go into the box before you start wiring; I was constantly disconnecting things I had forgotten to put in the container.
- Moisture does not get along well with amateur electrician work. Keep the controller away from heat and moisture (like above a water bath, sigh).

The Detailed Instructions

---

[53] Original post with chart of their data at http://qandabe.com/2011/revised-sous-vide-pid-calibration/.

- Lisa and Abe's original DIY immersion heat/circulator instructions: http://qandabe.com/2011/50-diy-sous-vide-immersion-heatercirculator/ and modified into a universal controller: http://qandabe.com/2011/70-diy-sous-vide-universal-controller/
- Scott Heimendinger's original immersion circulator instructions: http://seattlefoodgeek.com/2010/02/diy-sous-vide-heating-immersion-circulator-for-about-75/ (read the comments for tons of updates and trial and error from users)
- Dave Arnold's primer on how to use sous vide technology: http://www.cookingissues.com/primers/sous-vide/

Some Cheap Alternatives

When I spoke with ice expert Doug Shuntich about clear ice, he recommended two relatively cheap commercial temperature controllers. I haven't tested these, but Doug says: "The JCA419 is awesomely good. The TC can do cooling and warming simultaneously...dual function."

- Johnson Controls A419 Electronic Temperature Controller ($58 on Amazon)
- Control Products TC9102 Series Temperature Controllers ($50 on eBay)

How Much of a Difference Does Sous Vide Make?

I spoke to a number of scientists to try to find out what sort of quantifiable impact temperature has on infusion. Their answers were less concrete than I expected.

At a very basic level, we know that the rate of diffusion of flavor particles through water will increase in direct correlation to kelvin temperature. But that only accounts for about a 40% increase in diffusion from freezing to boiling. And we know that cinnamon tossed into a pot of boiling water will infuse much faster than cinnamon in freezing water—a good bit more than 40% faster, I'd venture.

What about solubility? Perhaps flavor compounds in cinnamon become more soluble? For example, consider sugar: at 0°C, about 180 grams of sugar can be dissolved in 100 grams of water. At 100C, that same 100g of water can dissolve 487 grams of sugar.[54] That's an increase of 270%. We're on the right track.

Other factors come into play. Heat weakens cell walls and accelerates osmosis through them. Enyzmatic reactions that would naturally occur within plant material happen much more quickly when heated. The viscosity of the solvent (water or alcohol) decreases. Unfortunately, I've found no systematic study of all these variables that can help me provide an estimate of how heat affects infusion.

What I did find was a comparison of the total mass of compounds extracted from three different types of teas at 70°C, 85°C, 100°C, and room temperature. The results varied by particular chemical extracted and by type of tea, but the rule of thumb: roughly **the same level of compounds were extracted in 4 minutes at 70°C as were extracted in 16 hours at 25°C.** Do some quick division, and you'll see that for tea, the difference of 45 degrees means a 200 times increase in infusion speed.

But why sous-vide?

Why not just heat everything up on the stove to 70°C or even higher and infuse that way? Because 70°C also happens to be the temperature at which plant cell walls—cellulose and pectin—start to break down. When this happens, any infusion will turn cloudy with pectin gels and become very difficult to clarify. The flavor profile of the infusion will also change because large molecules that would not have transferred through osmosis would be released. It's for this reason that the best infusing temperature for fresh ingredients is around 60°C and why precision temperature control comes in handy.

How to Make Clear Ice, Revisited

I explained in the "Consistently Freeze Crystal-Clear Ice" chapter that freezing clear ice depends on only one thing: precise temperature control. Specifically, freezing ice as close to the freezing temperature as possible. A few of you lucky folks will

---

[54] http://chestofbooks.com/food/science/Experimental-Cookery/The-Solubility-Of-The-Sugars.html

find that your dorm-style refrigerators already have a temperature zone perfect for this purpose.

For those of you who don't, simply repurpose the PID controller you built above to control your refrigerator. The basic instructions look like this:

- For the JLD612 PID controller, change the "R_d" setting on the PID controller to 1. This will set it to "cold" mode.
- Set the thermostat of the refrigerator to full blast.
- Tape the temperature probe onto a side wall of the refrigerator in the compartment where you want temperature to be controlled. I recommend the top shelf of the refrigerated section—that way, the freezer portion stays frozen and the refrigerated section stays cold. Make sure the probe is as close to your ice mold as possible—extreme temperature gradients can form in small refrigerators. If feasible, insulate the other shelves of the fridge with Styrofoam to mitigate temperature gradients.
- ***Very important*** change the control period parameter, O_t, to 10 seconds or more. This makes it so that the compressor must come on for at least 10 seconds at a time. The compressor can be damaged if it cycles too fast. Ice and refrigeration expert Doug Shuntich also told me that the optimal delay should be closer to 3 minutes, depending on the type of refrigerant your refrigerator uses. Using a 10-second delay, my temperatures fluctuated by about a degree, which was good enough for my purposes, but you may want to experiment with longer delays. Abe from QandAbe also says you can also try changing the P term in PID to 1% instead of 0.2% to compensate for the slower effect of a refrigerator as compared to a heating element.

I made this controller for a friend and used the case to a pair of racquetball goggles as the container.

This is the controller I currently use to drive my mini-fridge. Here, it's shown rigged up to a slow cooker.

The Cream Whipper:
An Unlikely Multi-Tasker

In early 2011, researchers at the University of Illinois recruited students to get drunk and take a test. No—this wasn't part of dare or a joke. The researchers were measuring the students' creative problem-solving ability. They confirmed the surprising truth: **drunk people are more creative—up to 40% more so than sober people.**[55]

The mechanism isn't entirely clear, but it seems that alcohol inhibits the activity of the frontal lobes of the brain—the areas responsible for sequential, rational problem-solving. With these areas subdued, the brain automatically looks for less likely, more "outside-the-box" solutions to problems.

Maybe that's what happened with the humble cream whipper. At first glance, an ISI[56] cream whipper would appear to have a simple function. It's all in the name, really. The device whips cream into... whipped cream. But as it would turn out, the ISI cream whipper can do more than just whip cream. Think outside the box.

Make Foams Out of Anything

First, a quick primer. In chemistry, a **dispersion** describes the evenly-spread mixing of a material into a liquid. Liquid-in-liquid dispersions (like vinaigrette) are **emulsions.** Solid-in-liquid dispersions (like coffee) are **suspensions.** Gas-in-liquid dispersions are **foams.** Other words for foams from the modernist cooking movement include **espuma** (which is just "foam" in Spanish) and **air,** which describe extremely light foams.

Whipped cream is a foam of air suspended in cream. (Cream is itself an emulsion of fat in water). The fat in the cream thickens the foam and gives it a silky mouth-feel. **Lecithins** act as **emulsifiers,** keeping everything together.

---

[55] Jarosz et al., *Uncorking the muse: Alcohol intoxication facilitates creative problem solving (2012).*
[56] Pronounced either "eye-ess-eye" or "eesee" depending on where you live.

There are plenty of different ways to make foams of varying textures. Below are some of my favorites.

#1: Beer Foam

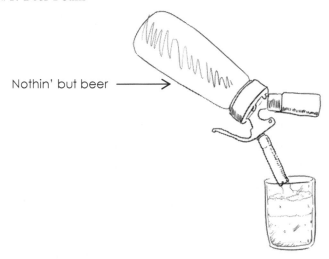

Nothin' but beer ⟶

This one's my favorite alternative use for the ISI. Beer contains naturally-occurring proteins and carbohydrates that give it a slightly smooth mouthfeel. With an ISI whipper, it's a simple trick to give any beer a rich Guinness-like foam. Next time a cocktail calls for a "float of champagne" try substituting a "foam of Bud Light" instead.

Here's a recipe, as an example:

Foamed Averna Stout Flip
Inspired by Frederic Yarm, Cocktail ~~Virgin~~ Slut

2 oz. Averna Amaro
2-3 dashes Angostura Bitters
1 Whole Egg

7 oz. Guinness Extra Stout (or other bitter stout)
1 oz. 1:1 Simple Syrup
0.05 g Xanthan Gum (optional)

Shake and strain the first three ingredients into a short highball glass.

If using xanthan gum, mix it with the simple syrup ahead of time. Carefully pour Beer and Simple Syrup into a pint-sized ISI whipper. Charge with one CO_2 canister and one N_2O canister. Shake after each charge. Upend the whipper and immerse its nozzle in the cocktail. Dispense foam until the highball glass is full. Garnish with freshly-grated nutmeg. Serve with a straw, stirring stick or spoon.

Note:

- I found that the Extra Stout didn't hold on to its carbonation well, which is why I recommended charging with CO_2 first. Not all beers will require this.
- I call for xanthan gum in this recipe to produce a slightly denser foam, but whether you think it's necessary depends on the beer and the desired mouthfeel of the final drink. Try foaming the beer by itself first to see what type of foam it forms.

#2: Egg Foams and Egg Substitutes

- Egg whites are powerful emulsifiers. To make a rich foam out of any syrup, combine 1 egg white (approx. 1 oz. liquid) for every 3 oz. other liquid.
- The best substitute for egg white is egg white powder. Use 2 tsp. powder and 2 tbsp. water for 1 oz. of egg white. Egg white powder is great for folks who are concerned about eating raw eggs and for batching, as it's easier to guarantee consistency. Raw eggs can vary slightly.
- Watch bartender Jamie Boudreau demonstrate how to make an elderflower foam with egg whites on his *Raising the Bar* on online cocktail video site Small

Screen Network. Look for the "Mexican Cloud Cocktail." Compare his recipe to the non-egg-white-based recipe for elderflower foam, mentioned below.

#3: Other Foaming Agents

I haven't done quite as much experimenting with these ingredients as I would have liked to, but here are a few ideas to get you started. For much more information and beautiful photos, check out the Molecular Recipes website, where you can also purchase food-safe geeky cocktail ingredients.

Martin Lersch's Hydrocolloid Recipe collection remains one of the best guides on how to use modern hydrocolloids. In it, he tests how much gelatin is needed to form a gel with alcohol:

Alcohol in Dish (%)	Gelatin Required (%)
0	1
5	1.8
10	2
15	2.2
20	2.4
30	2.8

Hydrocolloid Recipe Collection, pg. 81 via blog.khymos.org

Values given for 180-bloom gelatin. The concentrations listed above will allow you to create a gel, not a foam. Think of the ratios as the maximum theoretical useful amount of gelatin you can add to alcohol. To make a foam using gelatin, Molecular Recipes recommends using a scaling of about 1% in 16% ABV. Look on their website for the original recipe, under "Elderflower Foam" in the molecular mixology section. [57]

Molecular Recipes also carries the foaming agents Versawhip and Methycellulose. I've tested both, and I strongly prefer Methycellulose because Versawhip has a bit-

---

[57] ABV calculation assumes Chardonnay is 12% ABV. Link:
http://www.molecularrecipes.com/molecular-mixology/elderflower-foam/

ter, metallic aftertaste that I found overpowering. Methycellulose also forms foams much more quickly than Versawhip.

Here's an example of how to use Methylcellulose:

Lemon Drop Cocktail with Lemon-Lavender Foam

1.5 oz. Vodka
0.5 oz. 1:1 Simple Syrup
1 oz. Lemon Juice

1.25 g Methylcellulose
0.45 g Xanthan Gum
50 g Lemon Juice
50 g 1:1 Simple Syrup
10 g Crème de Violette (or lavender syrup)

To make the drink, shake and strain the first three ingredients into a large chilled champagne flute.

To make the foam, combine remaining ingredients and whip on high with an electric or stand mixer, or immersion blender, for about 3 minutes. Spoon the foam on top of the drink. Garnish the top of the foam with lemon zest and granulated sugar.

Notes:

- You'll notice from the recipe that I call for a scaling of 1.25% methylcellulose and 0.45% xanthan. To decrease the thickness of the foam, decrease the xanthan scaling.
- "Methylcellulose" is a generic name used to describe a wide variety of plant-derived hydrocolloids. I can only vouch for the specific brand and type I tested—Methylcellulose F50, provided by Molecular Recipes. Your results may vary.
- If you choose to use Versawhip, a scaling of 3% Versawhip and 0.45% xanthan produces a similar texture.
- If you have it, garnish with demerara sugar or another sugar with large flakes. Kosher salt makes an interesting contrast as well.

These are by no means the only way to form foams, but they work well for cocktails and are simple to make at home. See one other really cool way to make a foam in the "Odds and Ends" section, under "Permanent Aroma".

Extreme Carbonation

Don't waste money buying an ISI Soda Siphon. An ISI cream whipper will accept CO_2 cartridges. To carbonate soda in a cream whipper, simply pour the syrup and water into the metal carafe, screw on the head of the device, and charge with one to two CO_2 cartridges.

To dispense, first very slowly release the gas from the container with the nozzle, nozzle pointed to the sky. If liquid starts coming out of the nozzle, take a break and let the foam subside, or position a glass over the opening to catch the excess. Once all the gas is released, unscrew the top and gently pour out the soda.

I don't recommend using this technique on a regular basis because it takes a while to do correctly and because it costs a fortune. Using a cream whipper for carbonating does, however, come with one big benefit: pressure.

Whereas a SodaStream's regulator caps its maximum carbonation abilities at about 30 to 40 PSI, two charges with 8-gram CO_2 chargers on an ISI whipper equates to something like 200 PSI.[58] These high PSI's may be desirable when carbonating highly alcoholic mixtures, as CO_2 dissolves more readily in ethanol. I still wouldn't recommend doing this all the time, once again, for cost reasons, but it may be a technique worth exploring. Look for a follow-up on the blog.

---

[58] Based on my calculations using PV=nRT, assuming 550mL total volume in the carafe.

Rapid Infusion

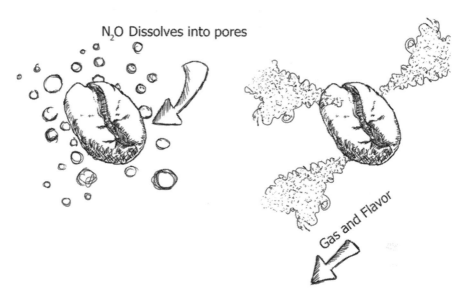

N$_2$O Dissolves into pores

Gas and Flavor

As we've discussed previously, hot infusions can be over 200 times faster than cold infusions due to a combination of diffusion, solubility, and enzymatic processes. Nitrogen-accelerated infusion functions through a different mechanism: physical agitation.

Let's say you load a coffee bean and some vodka into an ISI whipper. When you pressurize the canister with NO, the gas dissolves into the liquid solvents (water and ethanol) as well as the solid solute (the coffee bean). When you violently release the pressure on the canister a few minutes later, the nitrogen boils out of the bean, bringing with it the flavor oils of the coffee bean.

Online, I've seen folks use nitrogen-assisted infusion for everything from cinchona bark to cocoa nibs to bacon to dried herbs and spices. After running my own tests, I think the technique is best used with *fresh* herbs.

Almost all fresh herbs contain chlorophyll, a bitter chemical responsible both for photosynthesis and for most herbs' bright green color. When you muddle herbs or let them infuse for a long time, chlorophyll leeches into the alcohol and imparts an unpleasant taste. Rapid nitrogen infusion captures just the fresh notes of an herb because it doesn't give chlorophyll time to dissolve. Here's an example.

Basil-Infused Daiquiri

Inspired by Dave Arnold, Booker and Dax, New York, NY
Recipe adapted from StarChefs.com

For two drinks:
20 grams Thai Basil
4 oz. Flor de Cana White Rum
2 oz. Lime Juice
1.5 oz. 1:1 Simple Syrup
6 drops Saline Solution (1:10)

Combine Thai basil and rum in an ISI whipper. Charge with two N_2O canisters. Swirl lightly. Let sit for 1 minute. Discharge the gas. Strain the basil leaves from the infusion.

Combine remaining ingredients. Shake, then strain into a coupe glass to serve. Garnish with a leaf of basil that has been slapped between your hands to release the herb's oils.

Notes:

- This drink is a mash-up between two techniques that Dave Arnold developed. He usually makes this drink using liquid-nitrogen-muddled leaves of Thai basil. The result is a luscious and bright green drink that tastes strongly of basil. Here, I've replaced the muddled basil with basil-infused rum. It still tastes delicious, but the basil is much less pronounced and the drink ends up clear, not bright green.

- 20 grams of basil comes out to something like 30 or 40 leaves—a lot of basil is required for this drink.

What do I need to buy?

For any of the techniques covered in this chapter, you'll simply want a standard ½ pint- or 1 pint- sized aluminum ISI cream whipper and plenty of nitrogen and carbon dioxide chargers. The smaller whippers are better for home use because you can work with smaller quantities and use fewer chargers to achieve the same pressure.

DRINKS TO CONVERT THE COCKTAIL NOVICE

Some time ago, I went to a well-known cocktail bar in Washington D.C. with a group of friends. It was a busy Saturday night. As I browsed through the nightly cocktail offering, a list that boasted a drink made with a rare mescal alongside a grapefruit-heavy Negroni variant, two of my friends headed to the bar and asked for "something fruity," and "not too alcoholic." Moments later, they were back at the table, fluorescent tropical concoctions in hand.

You could argue that these girls were asking for it—that they ordered crappy cocktails and got exactly what they asked for. I tasted both drinks; one contained pineapple, orange juice, and a healthy serving of vodka. The other, ditto, but with some grenadine splashed in, apparently more for color than anything else. It made me sad.

Now contrast that evening with another experience I had:

I was out on date night with my wife at Comfort in Richmond, VA, once again on a busy Saturday night. We sat at the bar, the other standing-room only patrons jostling up behind us. My wife made her order—"something fruity," and "not too much alcohol." Bartender Mattias Hagglund was working the stick that night and he poured a simple, but extremely tasty drink. I don't remember the exact brands anymore, but here's the gist:

Something Fruity, Not Too Strong

1 oz. Sparkling Wine
1 oz. Homemade Grenadine
½ oz. Elderflower Liqueur
1 oz. Lemon Juice

Shake all ingredients except wine. Strain into coupe glass. Top with sparkling wine. Twist the oils of one lemon peel over the glass and discard the peel.

Homemade Grenadine

2 cups POM brand or similar quality Pomegranate Juice

Pour the juice into a Pyrex measuring cup and microwave on medium for 10 minutes, or until the syrup reduces down to the "1 cup" tick mark.

My wife said this was the best drink she'd ever had. Quality prosecco and homemade grenadine raised the complexity of this drink. It was delicately balanced and full of flavor, but still fruity and low-alcohol—as ordered. It was a perfect example of what a craft cocktail should be.

How many times in your home bar have you dealt with guests who say they "don't like cocktails" or that they only drink Vodka Cranberries or Rum-and-Cokes? This is the toughest crowd to please, so here are a few ideas on how to appease and even convert these folks.

Emphasize Familiar Flavors

As we learned at the outset of this book, most people dislike the taste of alcohol when they first encounter it. It usually takes several experiences to build up a spot in the brain where the taste of booze can find a home. It has to do with memory. We don't know what to expect when we first encounter ethanol, so we associate fear and anxiety with the introduction. With time, we learn that the taste of alcohol correlates with good times and easy conversation.

To help ease the beginning drinker into a world of new taste experiences, it's best to build off the flavor memories he or she already has.

Strawberry... Jam?

I'm not sure how exactly the strawberry daiquiri came to be, but the earliest mention I could find of one comes from the 1952 book "Electric Blender Recipes." Later works suggested the drink was concocted to show off then-new electric blender technology and pump up demand for frozen strawberries—another novelty at the time.

Born of industrial convenience, it wasn't long before the red-tinged slushie became a prepackaged delicacy, a "just add cheap booze!" sugar bomb that only hinted at strawberry flavor.

For my reinvented daiquiri, I used a classic Daiquiri proportion, but added a tablespoon of good-quality strawberry preserves. I added a few drops of orange flower water to simulate the grassy notes of fresh strawberries. The high acidity of the Daiquiri also helps to make the strawberries seem fresher.

Craft Strawberry Daiquiri

1.5 oz. White Rum
1 oz. Lime Juice
0.5 oz. 1:1 Simple Syrup
1 tbsp Strawberry Preserves
1-2 drops Orange Flower Water

Shake all ingredients with ice. Double strain into a chilled coupe glass. No garnish.

Notes:

- It's important to double-strain to get out all the seeds and fruit chunks that come in preserves.
- I use the 3" RSVP Endurance Conical Strainer, about $8 on Amazon.
- Orange flower water is available in most middle eastern supermarkets. If you can't find it, substitute ¼ oz. elderflower liqueur for ¼ oz. simple syrup to get that floral note again. I don't like rose water as a substitute for orange flower water—they are very different, in my opinion.
- Orange flower water is a hydrosol—an intensely-flavored water-based byproduct of essential oil production. See the chapter "Tinctures, Oils and Extracts" for more information.
- Feel free to sub in dry white wine for the rum to make this drink a low-ABV introduction to craft cocktails.
- It's easiest to literally use a tablespoon to scoop out the preserves.

Time Out: Strawberry Jam?! How is that "Craft"?

The drinks in this section are designed for the cocktail novice, but they also cater to the bartending novice. Fruit preserves are a great way to experiment with flavor without dropping lots of benjamins on fancy liqueurs and syrups.

In fact, here are few more reasons they're awesome:

- **You probably won't do better at home.** Fruit flavors do not dissolve readily into water. To incorporate fruit flavors into a cocktail, your best bet would be to make a liqueur or syrup, but the flavor of these would not be as concentrated as preserves.

- **They are balanced.** Preserves makers add just enough sugar to achieve the ideal acid-to-sugar balance. And that means it's usually ok to add them to a sour without mussing with the other components too much. Easy.

- **Texture comes included.** Try the strawberry daiquiri recipe. You'll notice that the drink ends up with an attractive, long-lasting foam and luscious mouthfeel. That's due to the naturally-occurring pectins in strawberries that act as thickeners. I wouldn't pair gomme syrup with fruit preserves for this reason as well.

Blueberries and "Freshness"

What does a fresh blueberry taste like? Like most berries, it contains elements of cleansing acidity as well as grassy and floral notes that we associate with "fresh." In fact, I'm always surprised how un-blueberry-like fresh blueberries taste compared to their baked-goods form, when they take on an unctuous, nutty sweetness and that pairs well butter and spices.

To emphasize the qualities of fresh blueberries using only blueberry preserves, I added orgeat, a French almond syrup that's incredibly easy to make (see my recipe for "Simply Awesome Orgeat" in the "Tiki Drinks" chapter) to amplify the blueberry's nutty notes. I then added some cucumber juice to pump up the aromas of freshness.

Blueberry-Cucumber Cooler

1 oz. Vodka
1 tbsp Blueberry Preserves
½ oz. Orgeat
½ oz. Lemon Juice
½ oz. Cucumber Juice
2 oz. Carbonated Water

Shake all ingredients except water with ice. Double strain over rocks into a highball glass. Top with carbonated water and stir to combine.

Notes:

- Don't be afraid to add a few drops of cayenne tincture (recipe in the next chapter) to this drink. Cucumber pairs very nicely with the tingly burn of pepper.

Cucumber, like many other fibrous vegetables, is incredibly annoying to strain. It inevitably ends up chunky or at least hazy and gross-looking. Here's the technique I settled on, after much trial and error:

Cryo-Juiced Cucumber
Inspired by Alex Talbot and Aki Kamozawa, IdeasinFood.com

2 medium Cucumbers

Slice the cucumbers thin, about 5 mm/slice, though precision doesn't matter much. Move the slices to a zip-top bag and place in the freezer. Once frozen, remove and let thaw at room temperature. When completely thawed, toss the bag back in the freezer and freeze again. Remove and thaw at room temperature. Pour the juice out of the bag.

Notes:

- Use standard supermarket-variety slicing cucumbers. English cucumbers make for better eating, but I found their juice both lacking in cucumber flavor and too salty.
- The cucumber solids make a terrific gazpacho.
- The second freeze is pretty important—in my tests, I almost doubled my yield after a second freeze.
- My friend Mike Betancourt says that cucumbers will go just fine through a commercial juicer, so that may be an option if you're willing to make an investment.

On Blackberries and Shortcuts

Carey Nershi knows what it's like to be a cocktail novice. The proprietor of the popular local-food blog *Reclaiming Provincial*, she is no novice to self-education. Since she started blogging in September 2010, she has taught herself web design, photography, and social media—not to mention cooking. So when cocktails began to pique her interest in March 2012, she bought all the good books and started learning. Her experiments have garnered her national attention and her recipes are perfect for the cocktail novice, as she was one herself just a few months ago. Here's one of her recipes.

Blackberry, Lemon, & Thyme Syrup

yield: approximately 3 cups of syrup, enough to make 6 cups of soda

1 cup Blackberries, slightly muddled (or chopped, if frozen)
1/2 cup Raspberries, slightly muddled (or chopped, if frozen)
1 dozen sprigs Fresh Thyme
zest and juice of 2 Lemons
2 tsp Pomegranate Molasses
1/4 cup Goney
1/2 cup Sugar
3 cups Water

Combine everything except for honey, sugar, and molasses in a saucepan. Bring to a boil, then reduce heat to low, cover, and let simmer for 5 minutes. Remove from heat and let sit for an hour or two, or until completely cooled. Once cooled, strain solids through a sieve lined with cheesecloth. Return liquid to sauce pan, place pan over medium heat, then add honey, sugar, and molasses, and stir until just dissolved. Remove from heat and let cool once again.

Carey's online persona blends the hyper-local with modern global connectivity. She experiments with only the freshest ideas and techniques, those not yet exploited by the mainstream, while using ingredients that are in season and from the area (Burlington, VT).

In many ways it breaks my heart to convert a fresh and local recipe into a simplified facsimile. But asking a cocktail novice to embrace the challenges of sourcing, processing, and blending fresh berries for a single drink would be like asking a dorm-room chef to butcher meat for lunch. I think the below recipe is delicious, but I also hope it inspires you to try the original if you get the chance.

Blackberry, Lemon, & Thyme Syrup (Simplified)
yield: approximately 1 cup of syrup, enough to make 4 cups of soda

3 oz. (6 tbsp) Blackberry Preserves
4 sprigs Fresh Thyme
zest and juice of 1 Lemon
1 tbsp Honey
40g Sugar
1/2 cup Water

Pour water into heat-proof container. Add thyme. Microwave on high until water barely boils. Let sit for 20 minutes. Remove thyme. Combine remaining ingredients.

Notes:

- The fresh ingredients release a large amount of water, so it's best to use 1 part syrup to 1 part carbonated water. For my simplified version, use a ratio of 1 part syrup to 3 parts carbonated water. For a delicious novice cocktail, mix 1 to 2 parts vodka to 4 parts finished soda. For a more complex drink, use Pimm's No. 1 Cup fruit liqueur instead of the vodka.
- Carey recommends mixing the syrup with water and carbonating everything in a SodaStream rather than adding the syrup to carbonated water. In fact, I would recommend adding the alcohol as well and carbonating the whole she-bang into a delicious highball.

On that note...

Bubbles Make a Good Mixer

According to the venerable and debaucherous cocktail hero Gary "Gaz" Regan, the highball has a simple definition:

> *Highballs are built in highball glasses; they call for a base spirit and a mixer, such as soda or water.*
>
> —The Joy of Mixology (2003), pg. 146

But simple beginnings often become celebrated obsessions, and so it has happened with the basic highball. In Japan, a simple whisky highball requires exactly 13½ clockwise stirs.[59] In Spain, an order for a "gin and tonic" is akin walking into a brewpub and ordering "a beer, please." You'll get blank stares and then barman will hand you a menu full of G&T variations.

The classic highball glass held just 8 ounces of liquid. And since we know that drinks were built to fit the glass in the old days, the perfect highball ratio should be a no brainer: 2 oz. spirit + 3 oz. mixer + ice, which should leave just about ½ oz. of room at the top of the glass. Of course, as palates vary, feel free to change ratios to suit.

Before getting into specific drinks, let's look at carbonated water in general and then tackle a few common highballs that can easily be super-charged (pun intended).

How to Carbonate Water—and Anything Else

For simple, no-fuss carbonation at home, you really can't beat the SodaStream carbonation system. Although the company has recently come out with a number of clever variations on their base product, the foundation remains the same.

---

[59] http://www.alcademics.com/2011/06/mizuwari-japanese-whisky-highball-ritual.html

As shown in the below illustration, a SodaStream "machine" is nothing more than a plastic shell that connects a pressurized bottle of carbon dioxide to a nozzle that connects to a plastic bottle. To make carbonated water, simply fill the plastic bottle with water and press the small bottom at the top of the unit. The carbon dioxide pumps into the water until a preset pressure is reached; a buzzing or whistling tells you when to release the button.

CO₂ Canister

SodaStream is adamant that you only carbonate water in the unit. This is because most other liquids have a tendency to foam. Foams are created when parts of a liquid form a matrix filled with gas above the body of the drink. In thick syrups, carbohydrates are the culprit. In sodas, emulsifying agents play a role. In wines and beers, proteins from yeast fermentation actually play a large part in creating this foam.[60] You can read more about how to use these facts to your advantage in the chapter "The Cream Whipper: An Unlikely Multitasker" in the "Hardware" section.

If you were to try to carbonate any of these liquids in a SodaStream, it's likely that the product would foam over when you released the gas. Sugar could then get trapped in the crevices of the device and mold could grow. And mold can be harm-

---

[60] Blasco et al., *Proteins influencing foam formation in wine and beer: the role of yeast (2011)*.

ful if ingested. That's why the SodaStream folks say not to carbonate anything but water.

With all that being said, I still do it.

Why? Because the SodaStream simply isn't a very powerful carbonation device. Since when you add seltzer water to syrup some of the bubbles escape, the only way to make a decently carbonated drink, is to add all of the components to the SodaStream and carbonate everything at once. Any of the carbonated drinks in this book can be made this way.

Some tips and warnings:
- If you're using hydrocolloids, it's probably best not to carbonate whatever you're making. Many hydrocolloids are used specifically to *make* foam, so it'd be counterproductive to try to mitigate their foam-creation capabilities.
- Most sodas are ok to carbonate if you're using at least a 3:1 water:syrup ratio. To be safe, always leave about two ounces of extra headspace at the top of the bottle.
- To prevent foaming, release the gas slowly by pulling the bottle toward you. Some foaming is inevitable, so make sure to wipe all the crevices of the device down with disinfectant after use. You could also use a hose—keep reading to see what I mean.

Now let's talk about wine.
Wine makes a great ingredient for novice drinkers; sparkling wines give even low-ABV drinks class and sophistication. But popping a bottle of bubbly for a few 1-3 oz. pours just doesn't make sense for home use. Luckily, it's easy enough to carbonate wine at home.

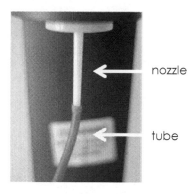

nozzle

tube

The process is surprisingly simple.

- If you can find them, get the 0.5-L bottles SodaStream makes. It will save you lots of CO_2.

- Try this technique with 4 oz. of wine to begin with—some wines foam more than others. Increase the amount if foaming doesn't become a problem.

- Cut a short length of silicone aquarium tubing,[61] and attach as shown in the preceding picture, this prevents CO_2 from agitating the wine as much, which helps keep bubbles from foaming out.

- Before carbonating, shoot a few blasts of CO_2 into the bottle to get rid of excess air.

- Get the wine cold. Carbon dioxide is more soluble in cold liquids.

- Clean the unit and tubing thoroughly after using. Submerge the device's nozzle in a little water as well to wash out any residual sugar that could have found its way up there. Sugar sitting for a long time can grow mold, and that's bad.

Seltzer water and sparkling wine are two of the most useful bubbly mixers you can have in your arsenal. A close third? Ginger beer.

---

[61] http://www.amazon.com/Elite-Silicone-Airline-Aquarium-10-Feet/dp/B0002AQI9A

Spicy Ginger Soda (that stays strong over time)

If you've ever tried making ginger beer or soda or ginger syrup, you've experienced this weird phenomenon: your concoction starts off spicy and gingery, but soon becomes tepid and plain. What's up with that?

As Harold McGee conveniently explains, [62] ginger contains gingerol, a fast-degrading chemical responsible for its trigeminal (spicy) bite. Luckily, gingerol behaves a lot like capsaicin, the stuff found in cayenne pepper. So why not replace ephemeral gingerol with long-lasting capsaicin?

---

[62] "Cooking reduces ginger pungency by transforming some bv and shogaols into zingerone, which is only slightly pungent and has a sweet-spicy aroma." McGee, Harold, On Food and Cooking (2007), pg. 426.

Long-Lasting Ginger Soda

1 lb. fresh Ginger, sliced
2 cups Water
440g Granulated Sugar (about 2 cups + 4 tbsp)
13 g Citric Acid (about 1 tbsp)
3/4 tsp Cayenne Tincture (see below)
Carbonated Water

Yields about 2 cups of syrup, or enough to make 16 servings of soda.

Peel the ginger with a small spoon (it doesn't have to be perfect) and slice into rounds. Add these to the water and simmer for about 20 minutes, uncovered. Your water should reduce down to about 1.25 cups. Strain the liquid out with a hand strainer.

Add the sugar and citric acid to the liquid and let rest at room temperature until all the sugar dissolves. This will take about 30 minutes. You can speed things up by shaking it a little.

Add the cayenne tincture a little at a time until you get the spice you want. I liked 3/4 tsp. Combine 1 to 2 oz. finished syrup with 7 oz. of soda water for a refreshing drink.

Normally, I recommend infusing ingredients at room temperature with the assistance of a blender or osmosis because many volatile flavor compounds are destroyed when heated. Ginger is different. The chemical that gives ginger its pungency, aptly named gingerol, degrades rapidly no matter how you store it. Also, I've tasted hot-infused and cold-infused ginger syrup side-by-side and the heated version tastes more ginger-y. This came as a complete shock, but facts are facts.

Saturated Cayenne Tincture

1 tbsp Cayenne Powder
1 oz. high-proof Grain Alcohol or Vodka

Combine, twiddle thumbs, strain. Yields about an ounce—enough to spice 2
batches of ginger soda.

Notes.

- Capsaicin, a non-polar molecular, dissolves readily in alcohol but not in water. The higher proof alcohol you use to make this tincture, the more capsaicin will leech out. This means that if you only have access to 80-proof vodka, you'll probably need to add more of the tincture to your ginger soda to achieve the same burn.

- A coffee strainer works well to strain this. The AeroPress® method (see the chapter on Filtration) would be overkill.

This spicy ginger soda is a versatile ingredient for many different drinks because it can be used in drinks calling for both ginger ale and ginger beer. This is because the "ginger ale" called for by many classic cocktails more closely resembled what is sold today as "ginger beer." And true ginger beer (the alcoholic, fermented type) doesn't actually play a large role in cocktails.

Some classic recipes using ginger soda:

- **Dark and Stormy.** 2 parts Gosling's Black Seal Rum, 3 parts Ginger Soda, Garnish with lime wedge.

- **Moscow Mule.** Same as above, but with vodka instead of rum.

- **Anejo Highball.** Credited to Dale Degroff. 3 parts Anejo Rum, 1 part orange curacao, 1 part lime juice, 4 parts ginger beer, a few dashes angostura bitters. Garnish with lime wheel and orange slice.

- **Shandy.** Beer+ginger soda. Not rocket surgery. Or is it...

Some simple variations on ideas we've already seen:

- 1 oz. ginger syrup, 1 oz. cucumber juice, 2 oz. water, 2 oz. light rum. Carbonate.

- 4 oz. Ginger soda, 1 oz. blackberry preserves 1.5 oz. Tequila

Taking it to the next level:

Dark and Stormy Shandy
Courtesy Gabriella Mlynarczyk, lalovingcup.com

1 1/2 oz. Brown-Butter-Washed Rum
1 oz. Ginger Syrup
1 oz. Lime Juice
2 oz. Pilsner, Lambic, or IPA Beer
a float of Dark Rum or Bourbon

Add everything to a shaker with ice except for beer and rum float. Strain into an ice-filled vessel of choice, top with the beer and the rum float.

Notes:
- To make Brown-Butter-Washed Rum, use the freeze-infusion technique (see the chapter "For Every Particle, a Filter" under "How to Filter Anything") with 1 stick of butter, browned in a saucepan, per cup of rum. Original recipe credit to Eben Freeman of Tailor restaurant, New York.
- **Gaby says:** plain rum can be used but the brown butter adds a lovely savory quality.

Next, let's talk about another ubiquitous highball—the Gin and Tonic.

Jeffrey Morgenthaler on Design, The Internet, and Repeal Day

Jeffrey Morgenthaler is the bar manager at Clyde Common in Portland, Oregon. He also writes at his popular eponymous blog, http://www.jeffreymorgenthaler.com, where he popularized the DIY Gin and Tonic, among other awesome recipes.

I love that not only are you a blogger, but you really take the time to develop your online presence.

I've been doing this from 2004-ish, and back then there really weren't that many people blogging about cocktails, so it was a lot easier back then to create a web presence than it is now. Now, new cocktail bloggers have to compete with so much other information out there.

Sure, but it seems like you have an above average handle on things like CSS, html, Wordpress, and web design.

Well, actually, the web design thing comes naturally because my degree was actually in design—architecture, specifically. And, I'm pretty old, so as far as the technical aspects, I started out early. I mean, I was learning HTML when it was HTML3, you know? And early in my career I actually started a little boutique web design firm with a friend of mine, so at one point I was pretty fluent in CSS and XHTML, though not so much anymore.

I'd venture that jeffreymorgenthaler.com ranks in the top three cocktail blogs in the world, if not higher. What were some of your personal highs and lows of blogging?

Wow, honestly, I'm not sure I can say there were any real lows. I mean, I take blogging seriously, but never so seriously that I get wrapped around the axle—I mean, I never really have a low in that way.

As far as the highs, I feel like I've had some pretty good ideas and it's really pretty neat when other people use those ideas. I mean, like, the tonic water's been pretty popular, and the ginger syrup. I get a kick when I walk into a bar I've never been to, and I'll taste their "house made ginger beer" and realize—oh hey, that's my recipe! That's cool.

But really, what I wanted to happen is what everyone who does this wants to happen, and that's to walk into a bar and get better-quality drinks. And I think that's happened, so I'm really happy.

You have a strong online presence and persona just due to the popularity of your blog. How has that affected your real-world life as a professional bartender?

Only positively, really. I mean, I started the blog when I was living in Eugene, which is a really small college town south of Portland, Oregon. I was bartending there, sure, but because I was able to get the word out over the internet, I was actually able to get a better job. I mean—I work at Clyde Common now and I didn't even apply for this job—they actually contacted me because they saw my work on the blog.

Very cool! I had no idea. Probably one of the reasons your recipes get so much traction is because they consistently seem to be so well-balanced. For example—you claim to make the "best Amaretto Sour in the World," and, after trying it, I agree. How did you know when you came upon the perfect recipe?

Actually, I was just talking shit with some friends one day—it wasn't really anything formal. We were talking about classy drinks that we like, and someone brought up the amaretto sour and how it's totally delicious, but totally gross. And I said that I bet I could make the best Amaretto Sour. How many iterations did it take? Maybe 2? It's not a really complicated drink and it's pretty clear what's wrong with it: it's not strong enough, it needs fresh ingredients, so I basically fixed those things and that was it.

You've also done a recipe for homemade tonic water that was very popular. What are you doing lately with tonic water?

When I took over Clyde Common, I didn't just want to do gin and housemade tonic, because a lot of places were already doing that. I did some research and learned that one of the big drinks in the Czech Republic is Becherovka, which is a bittersweet liqueur flavored with cinnamon and cloves from the Czech republic, so we did a variation on that. That was our approach, calling it Becherovka flavored with quinine syrup and lime juice.

The other thing to keep in mind with Gin and Tonics is the G&T culture of Spain. There are so many different types of Schweppes tonic waters in Spain. All different flavors, and all Schweppes brand. Lavender tonic is probably one of my favorites when I was over there. It was really cool. G&T's are my go-to airport/airplane drink. I'll drink one at home from time to time too.

And why do you feel so strongly about Repeal Day?[63]

It's simple, really. It's kind of the only drinking holiday that makes any sense to me. I was just reading about the repeal of prohibition and was like "hey, this should happen." I try to make it out to Washington D.C. every year to celebrate, because I feel that's the most appropriate way to do it.

The DIY Gin and Tonic

Simple Tonic Syrup
Inspired by Jeffrey Morgenthaler, Clyde Common, Portland, OR

Yield: about 2 cups syrup, or enough for 16 drinks.

40 g cut Cinchona Bark
1.5 cups Water
220 g Granulated Sugar
6.5 g Citric Acid (about 0.5 tbsp)

Heat 1.5 cups of water to a boil on the stove. Once the water is hot, add the cinchona bark, kill the heat, and let steep for 20 minutes, covered. Remove from heat and strain out the cinchona bark first using a fine mesh strainer and then a jury-rigged AeroPress®. Move the liquid into a tupperware container and combine with sugar and citric acid at room temperature. Shake. Once the sugar has dissolved fully, store the tonic syrup in the refrigerator.

---

[63] Check out www.repealday.com to see what I mean.

That is the most boring tonic recipe I've ever seen.

Deal with it. You're reading this recipe and thinking: What, no lemongrass? No allspice? Not even some citrus peels or juice? No. Why? Because the variations are too numerous to count. [64] And they are certainly all good. The recipe I've posted above is even simpler than Jeff's original recipe. [65]

Yes, you should consider adding some of your favorite modifiers to the syrup depending on the cocktail and the base spirit. But not before you try a Gin and Tonic plain. Personally, I was blown away by how the simple bitterness of cinchona brought out complexities and harmonies in the gin.

<u>Simple Gin and Tonic</u>

3 parts Carbonated Water
2 parts Gin
1 part Simple Tonic Syrup

Build over ice. Garnish with a lime wedge, if desired.

For a very different take on the Gin and Tonic, see "Orange-Gentiane Tonic" in the chapter "The Extra Mile: Obscure Herbs and Botanicals, Simplified."

I got some useful guidance on making my own tonic syrup early on from bartender Mattias Hagglund. Here's one of his excellent recipes:

---

[64] Some examples: http://www.thekitchn.com/gin-tonic-4-fresh-botanical-tw-148122
[65] http://www.jeffreymorgenthaler.com/2008/how-to-make-your-own-tonic-water/

Tonic Rancheros:
Courtesy Mattias Hagglund, Heritage, Richmond, VA

2 oz. Milagro Reposado Tequila
1 oz. House Tonic Syrup
1/2 oz. Lime Juice
1/4 oz. Agave Nectar

Add ice, shake and double strain into a collins glass. Top with 2 oz. seltzer, then fill with ice. Garnish with a lemon twist.

Mattias's notes:

- The Rancheros also works quite well if you infuse the tequila with jalapenos, or perhaps use some of the Bittermens Hellfire shrub or Bad Dog Barcraft Fire and Damnation Bitters. [**my note:**] Or maybe a drop of cayenne tincture?

"Neat" Cocktails

Neat typically refers to a undiluted shot of liquor served at room temperature while **straight up** *is usually used to describe a drink that's chilled with ice (shaken or stirred) and strained into a glass.*

Colleen Graham, About.com Guide to Cocktails

The below is an excerpt from an email my friend Pip Hanson sent me on the evolution of a drinker (bolding is mine).

Pip Hanson on Palate Adaptation

"Here's what I find myself noticing:

1. Drinkers are converted with something like an Aviation or a Southside.
2. They head into more "sophisticated" territory with a Last Word or Corpse Reviver—stuff with a little more complexity and less overt sweetness (although, really, the Last Word is almost dysfunctionally sweet). Drinks like bittered sours, amaro sours, etc.
3. They graduate into spirits-based drinks: the Martinez, maybe Manhattan variations and Martinis.
4. Finally they get into bitter drinks: spirits and bitters, in various forms. Negronis, Boulevardiers, etc. etc.
5. And at last... once they start to get used to the taste of Campari... **they stop drinking cocktails altogether** and start to gravitate toward plain spirits, because they're sick of the overpowering sweetness and overtness of cocktails. Single malt Scotch, rum, bourbon, what have you.

They start seeking out subtlety and complexity. The dirty little secret of amari is that they're super sweet, and bartenders get away with liking them because the bitter flavors mitigate the perception of sweetness—at least initially. After a while, suddenly Campari just tastes like cough syrup—and that's cool in its own way, but it just needs to be handled with that much more care.

So the question I find myself asking is: what do we make the drinker who has graduated beyond Boulevardiers? Do we lose them to single malt Scotch? Or is it possible to find drinks that they can still find intriguing and subtle? What would those drinks taste like?"

And Pip's not alone.

Every week, I listen to the Speakeasy radio show,[66] hosted by bartender Damon Boelte. Each show, he interviews a different bartender—most of whom are from New York, but many of whom hail from around the United States. The recurring theme? Most bartenders prefer a simple beer or whiskey after their shifts, not cocktails.

Granted, bartenders drink substantially more cocktails than most of their customers—but what happens if desensitization spreads like a virus to the general population? Is the "cocktail renaissance" doomed to be no more than another blip in cocktail history, a high point that will someday be excavated by the future's equivalent of a David Wondrich?

Maybe I'm being crazy. Maybe bartenders simply tire of mixing work with play. Sometimes even Michelin-starred chefs just want a hamburger, right?

But I think part of it has to do with the form factor of the cocktail. Do you know any wine enthusiasts who complain: "man, sometimes I just want some crappy table wine?" Or a Scotch lover who bores of Scotch over time? Me neither.

I'll admit it upfront: I don't have any easy answers for satisfying the "neat" crowd. No amount of wizardry is going to produce a cocktail even remotely approaching the complexity of a fine aged rum or Cognac.

So think of the following chapters as ideas for the curious neat-spirits lover. Or as a platform from which adventurous bartenders can tweak the ingredients that go into each drink.

---

[66] http://www.heritageradionetwork.com/programs/61-The-Speakeasy

A DIY Cold-Smoker for $20

Cardboard and duct tape—very classy.

Up until very recently, "nightlife" for human beings consisted of sitting around a fire, basking in its warmth and glow, enjoying the companionship of family. It's no wonder that the scent of smoke, the gaseous embodiment of fire, evokes feelings of contentment deeply rooted in our combined psyche.

There isn't a sound biological reason for why humans enjoy the taste of smoke. Nutritionally, smoke provides us with almost nothing.[67] Yet, the whole race seems to have acquired a taste for smoke, even become addicted to it. From salmon to barbecue brisket to bacon, there are few foods smoke doesn't seem to improve.

Given our long history of using smoke for culinary purposes, it should be clear that the Smoking Gun™ by PolyScience (famous for their immersion circulators and other high-end kitchen/lab equipment) doesn't offer the home cook any new process or concept. What it does is make an ancient technique more accessible.

---

[67] Though smoking foods does act as a natural preservative.

If you have the means, I definitely recommend you buy a proper PolyScience Smoking Gun™, since it looks like it's soundly constructed and probably easier to clean and use than my ~~ghetto~~ homemade version. But, if you only have $20 to spare, use these—

Step-by-Step Directions

Ingredients

These descriptions should point you in the right direction at your local hardware store, and I will post direct links for each item at the companion blog to this book.

- 1 Syba Battery Powered Handy Vacuum, $7.80
- 1/4" diameter vinyl or silicone tubing, $3.11 for 10 ft. (I measured this, and the outside diameter should measure about 3/8", but it's sold as 1/4" OD at hardware stores)
- 1 pipe bowl screen (get these from a local cigar shop or pharmacy), $1.99/5
- 1 1/4" barb x 1/4" FIP pipe adapter, $2.10
- 1 1/2" flex pipe tee joint, $0.57
- duct tape (Gorilla Glue brand tape works best)—hopefully you have some of this at home already.

Total cost: $15.57 + shipping and gas money

Directions

1. Remove mini-vacuum from package. See figure 1.
2. Cut the "blower" tube in half (this is optional, but I thought it was silly to have the pipe go out so long). See figure 2.
3. Insert half of the pipe into the "blow" end. It should only fit one way, so this *should* be self-explanatory.
4. Stuff one of the pipe screens into the barb/FIP adapter. It should just barely fit. This screen will keep burnt ash from getting down into the tubes and the vacuum. See figure 3.
5. Cut a small section of the vinyl tubing, then cut it lengthwise so that it becomes a flat piece of plastic. Wrap this around the barb end of the barb/FIP adapter. See figure 4.

6. Stuff the adapter with tubing into the top of T joint. The brass of the adapter gets hot; the vinyl insulates the rest of the smoker.

7. Cut a 1 foot section of tubing (or however long you want it).

8. Trim off one edge of the tubing at an angle. Stuff this end into the "blow" end of the smoker. Cutting the angle into the tube makes this easier. See figure 5.

9. Tape cardboard all over the thing to make it sturdy.

10. Tape off as many seals as possible to keep the smoke from escaping. See figure 6.

11. Tape off approximately half of the end of the T joint. Letting some air helps to propel the smoke out the blower tube. Let in too much and the "suck" end won't draw enough air through the fuel to generate smoke. Some trial and error may be required. Shown in figure 6.

Figure 1. Vacuum and parts that come with it. Figure 2. Cutting the "blower" tube in half.

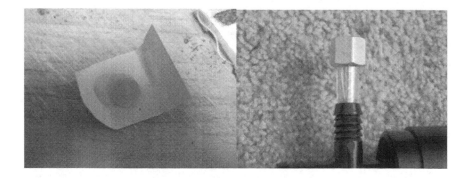

Figure 3. Smoke screens—5 for $2 bucks. Figure 4. Wrap some tubing around the barb to get a snug fit and insulate the plastic from heat.

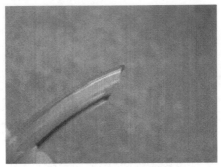

Figure 5. Cut the tubing at an angle—this will allow you to wedge it into the blower tube.

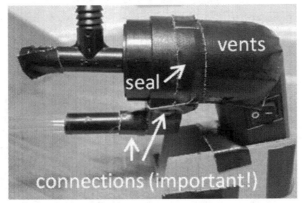

Figure 6. Tape these vents and seals to trap smoke.

See the smoker in action. Check the companion blog to this book for a video.

Some Important Warnings

- The metal of the pipe adapter gets HOT! Be careful.
- Since the adapter gets hot, it's best not to do more than one to two batches of smoke at a time. You really don't want the vinyl tubing that surrounds the adapter to melt.
- I've read concerns that the temperature of the smoke itself might cause deterioration of the plastic of the vacuum. I didn't experience this in my limited use, but I guess it might be possible. However, note that the professional PolyScience version of this cold smoker is probably made out of the same material, so I would guess that it's safe.

A Few Recipes

First off, here's one way to smoke a cocktail:

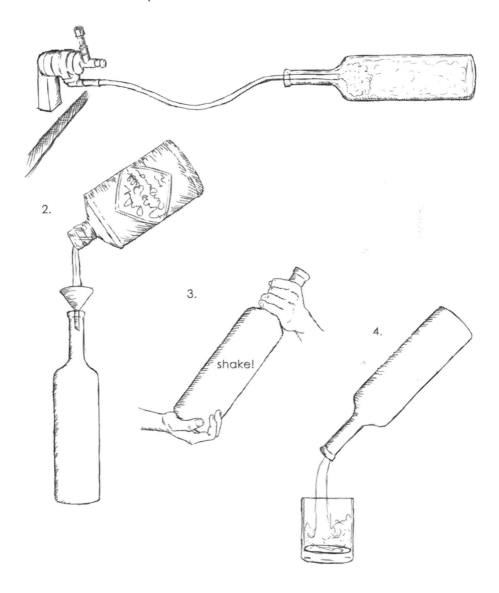

2.

3.

shake!

4.

Smoked Gin Neat

2 oz. Hendrick's Gin
1 pinch Dried Rosemary

Fill smoker with rosemary. Smoke 1 oz. gin. Let the smoked gin rest for 5 minutes. Combine with 1 oz. unsmoked gin. Sip and contemplate.

Notes:
- Think of this recipe not as a complete drink, but as an exercise in flavor. Note how the gin changes and mellows with smoke. Ask yourself: where does the rosemary end and smoke begin?

The next two recipes come from bartender Gabriella Mlynarczyk, previously of New York City's Woodson and Ford and now at Ink restaurant in Los Angeles. Her recently-established blog Loving Cup[68] showcases her behind-the-scenes experiments and thoughtfully-penned cocktail-themed stories. In Gabriella's own words:

"I am an artist—I studied painting and design as well as pastry and for years had it ingrained in me to look at everything from several perspectives, encouraged to dissect an idea and put it back together in as many variations as possible. It's now how my mind automatically works

I come from a family of cooks that believed in making everything from scratch, everything where possible and I like that this gives my work its own voice rather than being influenced by someone else's. Working with Chefs in several kitchens has been incredibly inspiring and exciting—it's how I have fun these days."

---

[68] http://www.lalovingcup.com/

Smoked Scotch Sour

Courtesy Gabriella Mlynarczyk, lalovingcup.com

1 1/2 oz. smoked Blended Scotch
1/2 oz. Melleti Amaro
1/2 oz. Lapsang Tea Simple Syrup
1 Egg White
1/2 oz. Orange Juice
1/2 oz. Lemon Juice
3 drops Chocolate or Mole Bitters.

Dry shake first, add ice, shake, strain into coupette, spritz drink with oil from an orange twist and discard the twist.

Notes:

- Gabriella uses a hotel pan, into which she pumps hickory smoke for one minute. I've found that an 8-oz. mason jar filled with smoke works well for 1.5 oz of Scotch.

- To make the Lapsang Tea Simple Syrup, make a double-strength tea using lapsang and hot water. Strain the liquid, then use as the water half in a 1:1 simple syrup.

Smoked Scotch Sour (left); Brown Butter Old Fashioned (right)

Brown Butter Old Fashioned
Courtesy Gabriella Mlynarczyk, lalovingcup.com

2 oz. Brown-Butter-Washed Bourbon
3/4 oz. Smoked Simple Syrup
3 drops green cardamom bitters
Orange Twist

In a chilled glass add simple syrup and bitters, muddle with a spoon as if you were making a Sazerac. Add bourbon and ice cubes, give a good stir to chill. Finish with flamed orange peel that is then dropped in the glass.

Notes:

- In case it isn't clear above, you're supposed to smoke the simple syrup with the cold-smoker gun. Oak works well.
- Gabriella makes her own cardamom bitters using green cardamom, gentian, over proof Wild Turkey bourbon and the sous vide method, but she says Scrappy's cardamom bitters makes a suitable substitute.
- A few wood chips goes a long way. A gram or two should be plenty to smoke a cocktail. Chips are available cheaply online at many retailers.

Don't want to go to the trouble of building a smoker? There's more than one way to smoke a drink:

Smoked Apple-Cinnamon Old Fashioned
Courtesy Jimmy Khaw, Cocktail Nerd

1 oz. Laird's Bonded Apple Brandy
1 oz. Cognac
0.25 oz. Cinnamon Syrup (see below)
1 Cinnamon Stick
2-3 dashes Angostura Bitters

Set a stick of cinnamon on fire and cover it with a chilled old fashioned glass. Stir the rest of the ingredients with ice. Turn the glass over and strain the drink in. Garnish with the burnt cinnamon stick.

Notes:

- It takes about 30 seconds to light the cinnamon stick to the point where it will smoke. Be patient.
- It's up to you whether you want to leave the burnt end of the stick up or douse it in the drink. I prefer to douse it.
- To make cinnamon syrup, simply steep 2-4 sticks of cinnamon per cup of hot water for 10 minutes, remove the sticks, and add sugar (by mass!) to make a 1:1 syrup.

Tinctures, Oils, and Extracts

The idea of adding flavor to straight spirits is not new. In 1884, Albert Barnes wrote the following in his book, *The Complete Bartender*:

> ### IMITATION OF SCOTCH WHISKEY.
>
> To 15 gallons of whiskey, add 3 gallons of pure Scotch whiskey, 1 ounce acetic acid, 1 quart of simple syrup. Mix well and add 25 drops of kreosote cut in ½ pint of alcohol; let stand a few days, when it will be ready for use.

The passage was not the only "imitation" presented. *The Complete Bartender* also includes imitations of Cognac, Bourbon, and multiple types of rum—18 recipes in all.

So maybe old-timer bartenders were trying to cut corners and pull a fast one on unsuspecting customers. But what if the powers of flavor they discovered were used for good rather than evil? First, let's discuss what flavor additives are available on the market today. After that, we'll look at some of the weird and wonderful things we can do with them.

A Glossary of Flavor Additives (and How to Use Them)

- **Extract.** Made by infusing botanicals into high-proof alcohol. For example, by steeping vanilla in overproof rum. Commercial extracts can also be made by adding high-proof alcohol to essential oils. Extracts can be added directly to cocktails (drop by drop) or spritzed over the top with an atomizer. Extracts can also be added to spirits to impart unique flavor characteristics (see following section).
- **Imitation Extract.** Exactly what it sounds like. Also made from high-proof alcohol, but the flavor component is synthetic: either a fragrance oil or a man-made recreation of an essential oil is added to the alcohol.
- **Essential Oil.** The undiluted aromatic oils of a spice, herb, or other botanical. Extremely difficult to use undiluted. A rough rule of thumb is to dilute one part essential oil in 100 parts high-proof alcohol. In my tests, 1 drop in 1 oz.

of 80-proof vodka was about right. Once diluted, you basically have an extract and can use it as you would any other extract. It is possible to add essential oils directly to large batches of spirits, but I haven't tried it.

- **Fragrance Oil.** Similar in composition and strength to essential oils, but whereas essential oils must be the pure distillation of a botanical, fragrance oils are usually synthetic. I think fragrance oils could someday be used to create a completely new gastronomic experience, but they would need to be tested first to ensure they are food-safe.
- **Tincture.** Basically the same thing as an extract, though "tincture" usually refers specifically to extracts made by combining a botanical with alcohol rather than extracts in which essential oils are added to ethanol. Compared to bitters: bitters are multiple botanicals dissolved in alcohol; tinctures are individual flavors. Some bitters producers develop bitters formulas by combining tinctures one by one.
- **Hydrosol.** The water-based byproduct of essential oil production. They are significantly less potent than essential oils and carry different aspects of a given flavor. There is no rule of thumb as to how strong each flavor will be. We already use orange flower water and rose petal water in cocktails; many others are available through herb distributors, such are Rose Mountain Herbs.
- **Oleoresin.** The naturally-occurring mixture of an essential oil into the hydrocarbons of its source plant material. Industrial oleoresins can either be taken directly from plant material or made by combining essential oil with resin. Used frequently in the food industry as a flavor ingredient because they are digestible. I haven't experimented with these at all because I haven't found a source online, but they look promising.
- **Essence.** A term I've heard thrown around to describe concentrated flavors, but it has no specific meaning.

What Flavors do Spirits Have?

Do you ever feel like punching people who describe spirits with words like "ripe currant," "mossy vanilla," or "strolling on a brackish beach and smelling a wood-burning stove in the distance?" Yeah, me too. A lot of these words come from marketing dorks who are more concerned that their taste descriptors match a product's packaging and target "demographic" than with what their product actually tastes like.

But what if some of those flavors really do exist?

I always wondered how a wine made with grapes from California could smell like bananas grown in Vietnam. As it would turn out, complex chemical reactions cause the formation of isoamyl acetate in wine—a chemical so banana-like it's also known as "banana oil".

In fact, even cheap, unaged distilled spirits can develop huge numbers of independently identifiable volatile flavor compounds. A list of common flavor compounds reads like an organic chemist's textbook: aldehydes, ketones, alcohols, esters, phenolics, and so on. The below chart lists a few of the most common and gives ideas for how to replicate those same flavors in mixed drinks.

Flavor	Chemical	Spirit	Imitation
Oak	Many	Aged Spirits	Oak extract
Cherry	Many	Aged Spirits	Cherry juice, extract, liqueur
Clove	Eugenol	Aged Spirits	Clove extract
Vanilla	Vanillin	Aged Spirits	Vanilla extract
Smoke/Roasted	Syringaldehyde	Aged Spirits	Wood aging, Liquid Smoke
Caramel	Many	Aged Spirits	Caramel extract; DIY Caramel
Smoke/Roasted	Guaiacol	Aged Spirits	Wood Aging, Liquid Smoke
Almond	Benzaldehyde	Aged Spirits	Almond extract
Cinnamon	Cinnamaldehyde	Aged Spirits	Cinnamon extract

Rancio[69]	Methyl Ketones	Cognac	Unknown
Natural, Juicy	Acetaldehyde	All	Unknown
Banana/Fruity	Amyl Acetate	All	Banana extract
Fruity	Ethyl Decanoate	Brandy, Rum	Fruit extracts
Floral	Linalool	Gin	Many, particularly coriander oil
Citrus	Citronellal	Gin	Citrus peels
Citrus	Limonene	Gin	Citrus peels, many other spices
Juniper	Pinene	Gin	Herbal extracts
Juniper, Citrus, Anise	Myrcene	Gin	Herbal extracts
Herbaceous	Terpinene	Gin	Herbal extracts
Funk	Ethyl Acetate	Rum	Rum extract
Peat Smoke	Phenols	Scotch	Peat extract
Coconut/Whisky	Whisky Ketone	Scotch	Whisky extract

References here.[70]

You'll notice that many of the signature flavors of spirits come from aging. For more on aging and why it develops so many complex flavors, see the next chapter.

Notes:

- In my tests, caramel extract was a far cry from using homemade caramel syrup. See the recipe later in this chapter.

---

[69] A term used to describe a signature flavor that develops only in Cognac and only after a minimum of 10 years of oak aging.

[70] Joachim and Schloss, The Science of Good Food (2008), pg. 216; Clutton and Evans, *The flavour constituents of gin (1978)*; Pino, *Characterization of rum using solid-phase microextraction with gas chromatography–mass spectrometry (2006)*; Watts et al, *Study of Aged Cognac Using Solid-Phase Microextraction and Partial Least-Squares Regression (2003)*.

- The company **Still Spirits** carries a whole line of flavor additives, from oak extract to concentrated peat. Unfortunately, I haven't tested them.

- Think using artificial flavorings or extracts will never be as good as the "real thing"? Consider Hendrick's Gin, generally respected as one of the top gins in the world. Both cucumber and rose petal essence are added to Hendrick's *after* distillation because their flavors do not distill well.

- Small quantities of cherry liqueur make a surprisingly delicious addition to almost any spirit where you want more of an aged taste. I particularly like Maraschino liqueur, which I've always felt had a slightly oxidized, smoky flavor.

Recipes

Burnt Sugar or Caramel Syrup

220g Granulated Sugar
1.5 cups Water

Heat the sugar in a stainless saucepan over medium heat. Stir with a chopstick every 30 seconds or so. You will see the sugar melt over time.[71] Once the sugar becomes fully liquid, it will become progressively darker very quickly.

For caramel syrup, the syrup is as hot as it needs to be once everything goes liquid. For burnt sugar syrup, the syrup is done when it starts smoking and releasing burnt odors.

Quickly pour in the water and stir rapidly. Be careful: the water will steam and may sputter a bit. Both the sugar and water will be crazy hot. If the sugar forms hard chunks, leave the pan with water on medium heat until everything combines into a smooth syrup.

Notes:

- Either burnt sugar syrup or caramel syrup can be used to tweak neat spirits, depending on how much you enjoy bitterness. I prefer the burnt sugar syrup.
- For bitters-making (see the chapter "Complex Bitters with Household Ingredients"), only burnt sugar syrup will have the bitterness you need.

---

[71] Technically, sugar doesn't melt, it dissociates.

Instant Aged Bourbon
Inspired by America's Test Kitchen[72]

2 oz. Cheap Bourbon
3 drops Vanilla Extract
1 drop Liquid Smoke
10 drops Dry Sherry
½ tsp Maraschino Liqueur

Combine. Serve neat.

Notes:

- I like the heavy smoke flavor of 1 drop smoke extract, but the original recipe would have you add something closer to ½ a drop, or 1 drop of a mixture of liquid smoke that has been diluted with equal parts water.

Instant Aged Rum

2 oz. Cheap Rum
1 barspoon Burnt Sugar Syrup
1 drop Orange Extract
2 drops Vanilla Extract
1 drop Banana Extract
1 drop Clove Extract
2 drops Taza Chocolate Extract

Combine, serve neat.

Notes:

- I like adding a drop of cayenne tincture to this as well. Why not?
- I like Taza Chocolate Extract because it contains a complex blend of spices. If you don't have it, substitute a few drops of crème de cacao instead.

---

[72] Available through http://www.cooksillustrated.com, though it's behind a paywall.

What's Really Going on With Aging

Tony Conigliaro stumbled upon aging by accident. He received a bottle of nearly centry-old Dubonnet from a friend and realized that the fortified wine had changed dramatically in the bottle.[73] He then asked the question: can a cocktail be aged in a bottle like wine? What Tony discovered began a major trend in the craft cocktail movement: **cocktails change drastically after a year or more in the bottle.**

Jeff Morgenthaler brought the idea to the United States and took it one step further by aging his cocktails in charred oak barrels—the same barrels used to age individual spirits. Few enthusiasts can afford a barrel of their own, but Tuthilltown Spirits will sell you a $10 kit that contains a nicely toasted chunk of oak barrel for straightforward "barrel-aging" at home.

For a fantastic overview of the science of barrel-aging cocktails, see Darcy O'Neil's post on the subject.[74] In this chapter, I'll focus on the one aspect of aging I think is least well understood in the context of aging cocktails: adsorption. But first, a primer of sorts.

The Chemistry of Aging (The Simple Version)

Aging spirits in oak imparts a complex and diverse range of flavors, including vanilla, clove, smoke, and caramel, among others. See the chart in the previous chapter for a small sampling.

Below is a basic summary of the processes that occur, assuming a standard 53-gallon barrel, dried, toasted or charred, and maintained in a temperature-controlled facility:

---

[73] http://tmagazine.blogs.nytimes.com/2010/06/01/case-study-vintage-cocktails/
[74] http://www.artofdrink.com/blog/barrel-aged-cocktails/

- Wood compounds infuse into spirits.
- Wood macromolecules (mostly hemicellulose) decompose; their products (mostly simple sugars) infuse into spirits.
- Compounds present in wood interact with each other; compounds present in spirits interact with each other. As these reactions occur, their products participate in follow-on reactions.
- Volatile compounds evaporate.
- Complex oxidization reactions occur, such as those that transform ethanol into fruity aldehydes and then into acetic acid.
- **Flavor compounds present in the spirit adsorb into the charred barrel surface.**

References: [75]

I won't discuss the majority of these processes here because they are extremely complex and not-well understood, at least in the context of aging cocktails. Instead, I'll point you to the most useful resource I've found from which you can extrapolate some conclusions: a master's thesis titled "Aging of Whiskey Spirits in Barrels of Non-Traditional Volume."

In the thesis, author John D. E. Jeffery compares the extraction of key flavor compounds in whiskies aged in 2, 3, 5, and 10-gallon barrels over the course of 200 days. His results show significant and unexpected variation between the samples. Furthermore, none of the smaller barrels successfully replicated whiskey that had been aged in a standard barrel for a longer time.

You could call John's work "unsuccessful," but that wouldn't be fair. His measurements constitute an important first step toward understanding and eventually controlling the complex interactions of aging. I recommend that those interested in the science read through his thesis, available online through the ProQuest database. Or you could simply taste John's work—he currently works as the master distiller at the award-winning Death's Door Spirits.

---

[75] Mosedale and Puech, *Wood maturation of distilled beverages (1998)*; Clyne et al., *The effect of cask charring on Scotch whisky maturation* (1993); And Darcy's post, which cites a number of other papers as well.

With all that background out of the way, let's move on to adsorption.

Adsorption: Theory and Practice

No book on "hacking cocktails" would be complete without a mention of the old water filter hack for salvaging bad vodka. It goes something like this:

1. Buy cheap vodka.
2. Pour vodka through standard charcoal-based water filter
3. End up with half-decent vodka.
4. Imbibe.

This hack works because commercial water filters use activated charcoal, the same stuff major distilleries filter their spirits with. But unlike other filters, activated charcoal works on the principles of adsorption, not clogging or jamming, like physical filters (see the chapter "For Every Particle, a Filter" for more information).

What is adsorption?

To make charcoal, you simply heat wood without burning it until all the volatiles cook off and a black lump remains. The carbon in this black lump has the unique ability to bond to many different types of other molecules. Here's the science:

> "Carbon atoms in charcoal can join together in a wide variety of forms with widely different electron distributions, meaning that it will have areas on its surface that are attractive to almost every kind of molecule. Once electrostatic attraction has pulled a molecule close to the surface of the carbon, van der Waals forces take over and hold it in place tightly. Charcoal also has millions of tiny pores in its structure, which create a very large surface area for adsorption to occur."[76]

---

[76] Nixon and McCaw, The Compleat Distiller (2001), pg 122.

"Activated" charcoal simply refers to charcoal that has been heat- or chemical-treated to increase the number of pores in charcoal or the electrostatic properties of those pores.

How do spirits-makers use adsorption?

For activated charcoal to do its work, it must stay in contact with a spirit for long enough that adsorption takes place. To guarantee that contact time, commercial producers force alcohol through column filters or filter beds. Think of your standard water filter as a column filter: you don't want to wait five minutes for a drink of water, so you use pressure to force the water through the charcoal. But whereas pore size and pressure are key to physical filtration methods, adsorption is a chemical process that relies on *time* and *surface area*.

So what?

If you're not worried about instant gratification, you can simply rest a spirit with charcoal for a set period of time and end up with a uniquely "filtered" drink without needing to force liquid through a column. Or would it be fair to call it "aged"? Here's an example of what I'm talking about:

Lincoln County
Courtesy of Pip Hanson, Marvel Bar, Minneapolis, MN

1000 ml Buffalo Trace Bourbon
600 ml Campari
400 ml Carpano Antica Sweet Vermouth
500 g Lump Charcoal

Break large pieces of charcoal into smaller nuggets to increase surface area exposure and place in a large sealable vessel. Pour bourbon, Campari and vermouth over charcoal. Cover and rest shielded from sunlight, agitating daily. After ten days, strain through a coffee filter. To serve, stir briskly over ice and strain into a chilled coupe glass.

Pip says:
- The charcoal absorbs some of the volatile aromatics and strips away some of the harshness of the bourbon, some of the syrupy flavors of the Campari, and

reveals caramel tones and previously hidden herbaceous notes. In practical terms, the cocktail becomes mellow and smooth, while also drawing a smoky character from the charcoal. It's pretty weird, but a surprising number of people love it.

- I experimented with using Brita® filters first, then Japanese hibachi charcoal, and now we're just using plain old Kentucky lump charcoal, propellant- and chemical-free.

Tips, Ideas, and Resources

I've already alluded to the fact that it's easy today to buy a pre-treated oak stave from **Tuthilltown Spirits.** According cocktail writer Donny O'Neill,[77] larger barrels can be purchased online from **Kegs & Barrels** and **Copper Fox Distillery.**

Alternatively, you can use some of the techniques in this book to simulate aging on a smaller scale. To impart smokiness, build a home-smoker and smoke the drink. To extract oak volatiles, use a kitchen torch to toast 5 g of oak chips per oz. of spirit and extract for 3 minutes with an ISI cream whipper. To try adsorption, bags of activated carbon in various mesh sizes are available dirt-cheap at distilling websites. You can think of mesh size as loosely correlating to "total surface area" of activated carbon. Mesh size determines how long a cocktail will need to be rested with the carbon to affect the desired changes.

---

[77] Original article: http://thehoochlife.com/2012/08/how-to-guide-to-diy-barrel-aged-cocktails/

IDEAS FOR BITTERS JUNKIES

It's amazing how fast trends in modern cocktails rise and fall. First, there was a revolt against any sort of dilution. At some point, bartenders weren't cool unless they were making house bitters and fresh liqueurs crafted from hard-to-find ingredients. Lately, there has been a healthy obsession with tiki culture, with drinks featuring pages-long ingredients lists.

One of the most polarizing trends has been bitter drinks: drinks featuring amari, bitters, bittered wines, etc. The trend is polarizing because not everyone loves bitterness. As I wrote about in the chapter "Why Some People Hate the Tates of Alcohol and What You Can Do About It", some people are born with an affinity for bitterness and others will develop a resilience to bitter drinks over time. But, some enthusiastic drinkers will never develop this preference, either due to genetics or some other factor.

With all that being said, I do think that bitter drinks are a real thing. The human tongue recognizes exactly one form of sweetness, one dimension of salt, a handful of "umami" dimensions, maybe ten different types of acidity, and over *three hundred* variations of bitterness. A single dash of cocktail bitters can add incomparable complexity to a drink.

Modern bitters makers genuinely understand how to balance bitters, which is why I've never tried my hand at formulating my own bitters at home—why bother, when so many great brands are available today? But if you're interested, definitely find yourself a copy of Brad Thomas Parsons' *Bitters: A Spirited History of a Classic Cure All*. It's packed with recipes and ideas for using bitters in interesting ways.

Even after reading Parsons' book and scouring the 915 replies in the eGullet thread "all about bitters," I still feel like I'm far from being an expert in bitters. So I thought I'd start this part of the book by talking to someone who is.

Selena Ahmed on Indigenous Bitters and Modern Extraction Methods

So you're an ethnobotanist? Tell me about that.

It's awesome! I get paid to travel around the world and study plants, or more specifically, how human cultures interact with plants. For the past 6 years I've been specifically focusing on teas in China, particularly the Yunnan province. But over the past ten years, I've worked in Morocco, the Amazon, the Himalayas, and India.

Wow, that *is* awesome.

Yeah, and while I have come across lots of interesting plants, I also discovered many indigenous ways of making bitters. It seems like there are almost as many extraction methods are there are plants. In most of the world, they're used as digestifs or for their medicinal properties. I also found that bitters were often mixed with other spirits, into what I would consider a cocktail, though that might not be what those cultures called it.

Is that experience what got you interested in making your own bitters?

So my partners, Rachel and Natalia also have their PhD's in botany and spent years in different countries collecting and studying plants. On top of that, we're all lab scientists. Actually, I've specifically been looking at how to extract the most phytochemicals out of tea, Rachel's done it with a bunch of plants in the polynice family, and Natalia works with the poppy family. In the course of that, I think we realized that we had developed a sort of "optimal extraction method". And of course, we all enjoy drinking cocktails, so making bitters seemed like a natural thing to do.

Can you share some information about your unique extraction process?

We started going down this track because of some different bioassays we were looking at.[78] We basically started off by playing around with the ratio of alcohol to plant material. We found that it does actually make a difference what your ratio is of grams of plant material to alcohol, as well as the proof of the alcohol that you're using.

It also matters how you do your extraction. For example we might sonicate[79] a material for 10 minutes and another for 30. Some things we extract under temperature. And then you can concentrate your extracts more, such as with a rotary evaporation. Our goal is to maximize the flavor compounds—both aroma compounds and bitter or bittersweet compounds like phenolics.

Do you make tinctures first or do you extract bitters as a whole?

So we actually made tinctures of 35 single species of plants and then we blended our formulas. When we blend, we'll taste mixtures first with the tips of our tongues, then envelop the entire mouth and, then finally we'll evaluate the finish. Our ingredients do each of those phases in different ways and then we blend them.

Research shows that a whole group of people, super-tasters, simply can't stand bitter flavors. Do you have any idea if you're a super taster and whether that affects your formulas at all?

That's interesting because it usually says people who are super tasters don't like bitter, right? I actually feel that I am a super taster and I really like bitter. In my class we ranked our tastes in order of preference and everybody put bitter last except for me and my co-instructor. We put bitter taste first and then at the end the students were like, well, you probably can't taste it. So, you have more tolerance for

---

[78] Bioassays are a lab procedure used to quantify the presence of target compounds in a plant material.

[79] The use of high-frequency sound waves to agitate biological material. In this case, that agitation causes flavors to infuse into the surrounding liquid.

it. I don't know. One big thing I've learned from my research is that in a lot of the communities I work in, bitter greens and bitter substances are consumed a lot more. It's just more part of the diet. Maybe I've just become more accustomed to it.

And on that note, do you think bitters necessarily have to be bitter?

No, I don't necessarily think they all have to be super bitter. We make our bitters to varying degrees of bitterness because we all like bitter. But when we develop recipes, we take into consideration their traditional use. Bitters are often seen as a tonic, like some sort of elixir for well-being. I've found that many communities' perception of bitterness is evolutionary—in our culture, people tend to have a repulsion to bitterness. Maybe that comes from some toxin in our past that was bitter. In other communities, people seem to have an evolutionary desire to have bitter substances, often as a way to cure or prevent diarrhea.

I guess what I'm trying to say is that the bitterness in our products is there because it serves a purpose. If bitters traditionally had a functional role, why not continue to see them that way?

Complex Bitters with Household Ingredients: What Works and What Doesn't

After my conversation with Selena Ahmed, I struck out to find bittering ingredients available at my local supermarket or pantry. I tried a number of different techniques.

Some things that didn't work:

- **Citrus peels.** Heat destroys the bitter compounds in fresh peels. For best results, dry the peels and make a tea of them. If you're going to do that, though, I figure you might as well purchase dried bitter orange peel, as it is quite a bit more bitter than supermarket variety peels.

- **Coffee.** Coffee can become very bitter, but extraction of coffee to target bitterness tended to extract many unpleasant off-flavors and acidity as well. Plus, the caffeine content gets pretty ridiculous.

- **Cocoa.** Delicious, but really really really hard to filter. Also not bitter enough to be worth it.

- **Chinese Bitter Melon.** Tried dehydrating and infusing it. Bitterness seems to evaporate with water content. Result was delicious, but not bitter. I assume you'd have to juice the melon to keep the bitter compounds intact. Too lazy.

- **Beer Syrup.** This can be delicious when done right, but I found that any reduced beer had significant acid notes that prevented it from being used as a singular bittering ingredient.

- **Cranberries.** Cranberries certainly taste bitter when they're not sweetened, but they also taste acidic and tannic. The bitterness gets lost.

Here's what worked:

- **Oversteeped tea.** I love this idea for a number of reasons. Tea is an almost universal drink, and well-recognized for its health benefits. As it would turn out, when you steep tea for so long that bitter and tannic flavors come out, you also extract extra phytonutrients—particularly polyphenols.[80]

- **Caramel Syrup.** Caramelization is a type of *browning* reaction (the other is *Maillard*) through which simple molecules—in this case, the disaccharide sucrose—are transformed through heat into complex aromatic compounds, many of which contain a bitter component. See the recipe for Burnt Sugar Syrup in the chapter "Tinctures, Oils, and Extracts."

Oversteeped Tea

2 filterbags Tea (or about 2 teaspoons Loose-Leaf Tea)
8 oz. Water

Simmer the tea in the water until the liquid reduces by half, approximately 10 minutes. Make sure to squeeze the filter bags of their remaining goodness. Store in the refrigerator; should keep for a long time due to the antioxidative properties of tea, though I haven't tested shelf life.

Note:
- This tea extraction technique works with any tea, including green teas. The bergamot of Earl Grey tea works well in the below recipe. Both green and black teas pair well with gin as well as acid-forward wines, such as vermouth and sherry.

---

[80] A "phytonutrient" is any compound found in plants that is believed to be good for human health. Polyphenols are believed to have antioxidative properties.

Teagroni

1 oz. Gin (Bombay Sapphire)
1 oz. Sweet Vermouth (Noilly Prat)
1 oz. Oversteeped Tea
1 barspoon (1/8 oz.) Honey

Heat the honey and tea extract in the microwave ahead of time to dissolve the honey. Stir all ingredients with ice. Garnish with orange twist or spritz of orange extract.

Note:

- This drink is a riff on the classic bitter drink, the Negroni, but with these proportions it comes out lighter and more refreshing. I prefer the drink this way; to make a more traditional bitter drink, use 1.5 oz. oversteeped tea and 0.5 oz. vermouth.

Tasting, Sipping… Chugging Bitters

In 2010, I was hanging out with bartender John Gertsen at an event in Cambridge, Massachusetts. As the night went on, the pace of the drinking accelerated, as was likely to happen at events such as this one. The idea of taking shots soon materialized, but the bar was only stocked with Crème de Cassis, soda water, and bitters. Not one to become discouraged, John smoothly popped the cap off a 10-oz. bottle of Angostura and began to dole out shots.

My face revealed my skepticism. If it had been a sentence, it would have read "are you shitting me?" But after John downed his glass and poured another, my manhood slapped me in the face and I emptied the inky black medicine down the hatch. It was, surprisingly, delicious. I was hooked.

Sure, most people only need a dash or two of bitters to round out a drink, but bitters junkies are not most people and I'm proud to say I'm one of them. Although most nights a glass of Averna satisfies my cravings, sometimes it takes a little bit more. Sometimes I reach for the Fernet. Other times, I find myself longing to re-live that first shot of Angostura.

Back in 2007, Jamie Boudreau came up with a makeshift recipe for Amer Picon (cleverly named "Amer Boudreau") that combined the amaro[81] Ramazzotti with orange extract and nearly a full bottle of orange bitters. Reflecting on the recipe, it occurred to me that most potable bitters and aromatized spirits (amari, aperitifs, digestifs, and the like) contain the same botanicals found in bitters, only in different concentrations.

I went on a quest to find out which bitters make for the best solo drinking. Below are some of the ideas that I think worked pretty decently. I apologize if my notes are a little excited at times—I was taking shots all night, after all.

Which Bitters are Most Potable?

- **Angostura.** Delicious on its own. Tingly, refreshing, sweet, astringent. Makes a great shot. However, you might as well save some money and drink fernet instead; it has a similar profile.
- **Regan's Orange.** Too intense on its own to make a good drink, but can be mixed into an amazing aperitif. See recipe, to follow.
- **Underberg.** Anise, clove, cinnamon. Smells sweet, inviting on its own. Slightly woody. A tad too bitter to sip. Tannic. Tastes of caramel and vanilla, once you get past the tannin. But the tannin is pretty strong. If you shoot it, the tannin isn't as noticeable. Very nice burn in the back of the throat, opens up some citrus notes. Also get some chocolate, distinctly sweet. REALLY good as a shot. Alternatively, see the recipe for "The Rejuvenator" at the end of this chapter.
- **Bitter Truth Xocolatl Mole Chocolate Bitters.** Really bitter on their own. Add an equal part of 1:1 simple syrup and 2 drops saline/oz. to create a bitter chocolate liqueur suitable for mixing. This brand tends to make their bitters with a strong aftertaste and not much sugar to offset the bitter flavors. I couldn't find a good way to make an aperitif-style liqueur worth sipping.

---

[81] A style of Italian bitter herbal liqueur.

Regan's Elixir

1 oz. Regan's Orange Bitters
1 oz. 1:1 Simple Syrup
1 oz. Dry Sherry (or other dry, acidic wine)
3 drops Saturated Saline Solution

Combine ingredients and serve as an aperitif over ice. The acidity of the wine is important, because it provides body that is necessary to complement the citrus high-notes of the orange bitters. Malic or tartaric acid can be used to adjust acidity. I found that the saline solution helped mitigate any bitter aftertaste.

- **Fernet Branca.** Delicious as a shot or sipped from a really cute little glass, like Alfred did in *Dark Knight Rises*.

- **Peychaud's.** Very different from the other bitters tested. It tastes more like an anisette than a traditional bitters. In fact, you can combine 2 parts Peychaud's with 1 part 1:1 simple syrup to produce a respectable anisette. But, really, no matter how much I tweaked it, Peychaud's just didn't taste as interesting to me as a decent absinthe. I guess this makes sense, since absinthe contains many botanicals also found in bitters, but it made me wonder—is there really a point to including both Absinthe and Peychaud's in a drink like the Sazerac?

- **Bittermens Boston Bittahs.** This is the only bitters I tested with an interesting spicy note that only appeared when I was trying it as a drink rather than as a bitters. 2 parts bitters to 1 part 1:1 simple syrup worked best, but even then the combination was a little syrupy for my tastes. I would recommend adding 1 part dry, light white wine and seeing how that works.

- **Dr. Adam Elmigirab's: Dandelion & Burdock Bitters | Aphrodite Bitters.** These bitters are on a whole different level from anything else I tasted. They are both easily potable straight from the bottle. The dandelion and burdock bitters taste slightly milder and sweeter, while the aphrodite bitters have a chocolate note and finish with a bitter aftertaste. Combining equal parts of these two bitters makes an amazing drink over ice or at room temperature. However, I now know to add more of these bitters to mixed drinks than I would use, say, angostura, due to their milder demeanors.

- **Fee Brothers Orange Bitters.** Another informative learning point. These orange bitters taste more like orange extract than a true orange bitters. While they were fresh and orange-y and slightly bitter, no amount of tweaking would have produced an orange aperitif worth drinking from these. This Fee Brothers product is best used to add a citrus note to other components.

Big important lesson learned. Although this experiment started off as an effort to make a fake amaro, it ended up being an education in bitters. Tasting through the different bitters drop by drop made me realize how very different each brand is. This is now my go-to way of tasting a new bottle of bitters and I would highly recommend you try it with any bitters you buy.

Recipes with Bitters

This one's pretty amazing—try it at least once:

Better Bitter Beer

Courtesy John Rutherford, Observational Gastrophysics

1 12-oz. can Pabst Blue Ribbon Beer
8-12 dashes Angostura Bitters

Gently stir to combine. Drink without a hint of irony.

Notes:
- I like PBR just fine on its own, but adding bitters to it completely changes the flavor profile. The beer gets a huge boost in aroma and complexity.
- I'm also partial to using a whole bottle of Underberg instead of Angostura. It's freaking delicious, but a little less convenient than simply dashing Angostura.
- John also recommends trying Jerry Thomas Decanter Bitters.

Notes:

- I love that Mattias calls for 2 dashes of Angostura in this recipe. Talk about icing on the cake.

How Much is a "Dash," Anyway?

Here's a fun twitter exchange I decided to save:

Ruhlman @ruhlman   14 Apr
@BTParsons if you're going to be an awardwinning expert at something almost always measured in dashes, youre the one to define what it is!

James Gordon @jrgordon13   14 Apr
@ruhlman @btparsons Thought I remember reading somewhere that a 'dash' is 6 drops from an eyedropper. Still, it'd be nice to know for sure!

Brad Thomas Parsons @BTParsons   14 Apr
@jrgordon13 @ruhlman 5 drops from eyedropper style bitters bottle equals a "dash." I believe Dave Arnold @CookingIssues has weighed a dash.

Dave Arnold @CookingIssues   14 Apr
@BTParsons I have measured it, but my data is back at the bar. I believe it is 17 American drops to the ml. Too much wine to remember.

Dave Arnold @CookingIssues   17 Apr
@BTParsons @ruhlman twitter not good format for discussion of drop size but I will do a multi-tweet. Ango bitters density .94 g/ml

Dave Arnold @CookingIssues   17 Apr
@ruhlman @BTParsons (50 dash average) ango from bottle: .68
g .72 ml per dash. @cocktailkingdom bitters bottle ango .43g .45
ml/dash

Dave Arnold @CookingIssues   17 Apr
@ruhlman @BTParsons @cocktailkingdom half-dash bottle an-
go .18g .19 ml/ dash. Eyedropper: .25 g/ .27ml/dash

frogprincesse @frogprincesse   17 Apr
@CookingIssues @ruhlman @BTParsons @cocktailkingdom How
many Ango bottles did you test this on? I noticed huge variations
between bottles

Dave Arnold @CookingIssues   17 Apr
@frogprincesse @ruhlman @btparsons @cocktailkingdom I only
tested one bottle (the large size). I'll try another.

Legend

@jrgordon13: PhD Student at Wheaton College in Illinois

@ruhlman: Michael Ruhlman, author of over a dozen top-selling influential
books about food and cooking

@BTParsons: Author of the definitive modern book on bitters.

@cookingissues: Director of Culinary Technology at the International Culinary Center; owner of Booker & Dax bar in NYC.

@frogprincesse: a Paris-Native, San Diego-based chemist with over 1,350
posts on food and cocktails at eGullet.

@cocktailkingdom: New York City-based proprietor of cocktail accessories and
ingredients.

And just in case you missed it, here's the translation:

- All tests were run using Angostura bitters, which have a density of 0.94 g/mL.
  Other bitters may have different densities, which would change the results.

- The Angostura bottle releases 0.72 mL per "dash." A bitters bottle from Cocktail Kingdom registers either 0.45 mL or 0.19 mL per dash, depending on the
  particular bottle you use. A standard eyedropper deposits 0.27 mL per drop.

- This means that 10 dashes from an Angostura bottle equals a 0.25 oz. and
  there are about 8 drops of angostura for every 3 dashes.

The Extra Mile: Obscure Herbs and Botanicals, Simplified

Spending a few solid hours tasting through my bitters collection really made me appreciate the complexity that goes into each bottle. The idea of emulating such masterpieces can be intimidating, as it should be. To start experimenting with bitters by trying to recreate something like Angostura would be akin to an art student learning to paint by copying da Vinci.

Great bitters are complex, but that doesn't mean playing with a single ingredient can't also be worthwhile. Here are some tasting notes and examples to start you off with experimentation.

My thanks go to Eva Marie Kosmas who tasted through every one of these ingredients with me. The final notes are a mash-up of our two experiences. For much more information and awesome pictures of making bitters, you should check out her posts on making bitters at http://www.adventures-in-cooking.com/.

Tasting Notes

Each ingredient was allowed to steep in 80 proof vodka. I did my tastings after one day, Eva tasted at 1 hour, 1 day, and 1 week. I also made a tea of each ingredient with hot water to see how the flavors changed. As a general rule of thumb, hot water extracts more bitterness from these botanicals, while cool alcohol extracts more of the aromatic components. Bear that in mind when making things like alternative tonic waters (see recipe at the end of this chapter).

- **Cinchona.** Clean bitterness, floral and woodsy. One of the few that I enjoyed enough without sugar to taste several times just for funsies.
- **Bitter Orange.** Orange, tart, citrusy. Another clean bitterness, although one of the weakest in terms of pure bitterness. Starts off tart and citrusy; bitterness becomes more pronounced after day 1. After a week the flavors are strong and fresh.

- **Angelica.** Complex, woody, very front of tongue, the bitterness is somewhat unpleasant, unlike cinchona or bitter orange. Tastes of celery, fennel, and cloves. After a week, develops a parsley character.
- **Gentian.** Intense, deep, slightly numbing and lasting bitterness. Definitely a trigeminal note in addition to bitterness. Woody. Very delicious.
- **Wormwood.** Minty, only slightly bitter compared to the other bittering agents, with an addictive taste. After an hour, it tastes of dill with some of the herbal notes of green tea. After a day, the bitterness becomes more pronounced, and after a week the flavor tastes almost exactly like dill pickles.
- **Centaury.** After an hour, centaury is warm and earthy like black tea, with a hint of coriander and grass. After a day, it tastes like extremely bitter tea, not particularly delicious, but seriously bitter. After a week, it develops a mossy flavor in a nice way. Tastes much better infused in alcohol than in water. In hot water, the bitterness gets extremely intense.
- **Licorice Root.** The flavor is aggressive and tangy at first but mellows out into more an earthy and sweet taste. After a week, a definite trigeminal sensation is present as well.
- **Betel Nut.** Think nutmeg. After an hour, the taste is subtly sweet, with hints of nutmeg and licorice. After a day, a gingerbread character develops. After a week, the subtlety of the shorter infusion is overshadowed by a strong licorice character.
- **Dandelion.** I only managed to get my hands on dandelion extract because I read that the extract uses fresh dandelions and fresh dandelions are far superior to dried. Dandelion extract has a mild, earthy flavor that reminded me of chocolate but wasn't very bitter at all.
- **Untested.** A few more bittering agents we never go around to: elecampane, orris, blessed thistle, calamus, hops. Please let me know if you've tried them.

Recipes

Breath of a Bitter Tune

Courtesy Andrew Cameron, originally by Marco Nunes, Canvas Club, Woolloongabba, Australia

40 mL Absinthe
15 mL Triple Sec
20 mL Passionfruit Wormwood Syrup
Cocoa Nibs
Kosher Salt

A few hours before service, grind the cocoa nibs until they are almost but not quite powder. Combine with salt at a rough 2:1 cocoa:salt ratio. To rim the glass, pour some triple sec into a shallow dish and gently roll the rim of a highball glass in it at a 25° angle to parallel. Repeat the motion in a shallow dish of the cocoa/salt combination. Let rest for a few hours to let the triple sec dry.

To make the drink, combine first three ingredients and carbonate. Pour into a cocoa-and-salt-rimmed highball glass over ice.

Passionfruit Wormwood Syrup

2 barspoons Cut Wormwood
250 mL Water
500 g Sugar
250 g Passionfruit Pulp

Heat the water and infuse the wormwood in it for about 5 minutes to make a tea. Combine the tea with the sugar and passionfruit pulp.

Notes:
- The original recipe calls for Koruna Absinthe; I used St. George Absinthe.
- This recipe's really tough to get right, but it's totally worth it if you can. The cocoa nibs and salt are crucial. In fact, I left a little dish of those two ingredi-

ents on the table next to me while I sipped and found myself dipping my fingers into it again and again.

- Passionfruit pulp can be difficult to find in the United States. I found that guava makes an acceptable substitute. If you use juice, I would recommend simply brewing the wormwood tea in hot juice, then reducing the tea to ¾ or ½ total volume.
- You'll know you have the right balance when the final drink stops tasting like "absinthe mixed with triple sec" and the slight funk of passionfruit/guava starts coming through. Then take a little taste of cocoa, and—awesome.

When I was playing was Gin and Tonic's, I always wondered "do we have to use cinchona?" No, we do not.

Orange-Gentiane Tonic
Yield: about 2 cups syrup, or enough for 16 drinks.

30 g Gentiane
10 g Bitter Orange Peel
1.5 cups Water
220 g Granulated Sugar
4 g Malic Acid

Heat 1.5 cups of water to a boil on the stove. Once the water is hot, add the botanicals, kill the heat, and let steep for 20 minutes, covered. Remove from heat and strain out the solids first using a fine mesh strainer and then a jury-rigged Aero-Press®. Move the liquid into a Tupperware container and combine with sugar and citric acid at room temperature. Shake. Once the sugar has dissolved fully, store the syrup in the refrigerator.

Notes
- The malic acid gives a G&T made with this tonic a refreshing fruity flavor that confuses the palate when it mixes with the bitter orange aroma.
- With this formulation, I thought a hefty squeeze of lime was necessary. Feel free to try increasing the malic acid content to 6 grams.

THE CLASSICS, HACKED

I've known nothing but progress during my brief tenure on Earth. Every year, a new invention announces itself and the past year's marvels fade into memory. I have been conditioned to expect that the human condition always improves, but such has not always been the case.

Let's look at an example: As early as the 300s BC, the Greek philosopher Aristotle came tantalizingly close to discovering distillation, the chemical process that converts wine into spirits. According to historians, the centuries after Aristotle's death were "enlightened" period of progress because the Romans and Han Chinese developed a myriad of advances in mathematics, education, and technology. But I'm not sure if I'd agree. I'd argue it wasn't until the 1400s that we truly started making progress again. And by progress I mean someone started selling distilled spirits as shots in Germany, around the 15th century.[82]

Why the history lesson? To illustrate an important point: although things have generally gotten better throughout most of modern history, that has not always been the case and cocktails are an unfortunate example. The reason why "classic cocktail" seems synonymous with "delicious cocktail" today is because a drink created one hundred years ago is likely to be better balanced than a drink created thirty years ago.

Why cocktails developed as they did has to do with laws, ingredients, bar culture, and all manner of other things not worth discussing here, but the classics are classic for a reason. [83]

---

[82] The process of distillation itself was discovered around the 8th century, and there's evidence of distilled spirits being drunk in the 12th century, but I'm giving credit here to the invention of shots as a major milestone ☺.

[83] See Drink, a Cultural History by Iain Gately, and The Prohibition Hangover: Alcohol in America, from Demon Rum to Cult Cabernet by Garrett Peck.

Note:

In the past three chapters, I've gone over techniques and recipes to deal with your special case dinner party guests—the outliers who need unique treatment. The rest of this book is for everyone else. These are the drinks every home bartender should be familiar with because they are classics *for a reason*. With that being said, you'll notice I've omitted many popular drinks, both modern and classic. I didn't mean this as an insult to any particular cocktail recipe, but simply for the sake of space.

Old-Fashioned vs. Sazerac vs. Martinez: A Visual Analysis of Cocktail Formulas

The Old-Fashioned Cocktail is the only cocktail I can think of that named itself. It's widely regarded as the world's first cocktail. And while that may be technically true (a "cocktail" at the time was defined simply as spirits, sugar, bitters, and water), the drink that we would think of as a cocktail today—spirits mixed with other tasty stuff—existed for over one hundred years before the Old-Fashioned came into existence.

The Fish House Punch is one of the cocktails that predates the Old-Fashioned and I discovered it in Melbourne, Australia. Before I visited Melbourne, I polled friends and fellow cocktails geeks about the one bar where I should go to for great cocktails. The answers all pointed to the bar 1806, an establishment known for a menu that spans the history of the mixed drink (1806 is the year the cocktail is generally recognized to have been invented in). It was there, over a Mai Tai followed by an Aviation, that I asked the question: how have cocktails changed over the years?

The following chart, based off of recipes from 1806's bar menu, is the answer I came up with.

The Horizontal Approach: Cocktail Formulas over Time

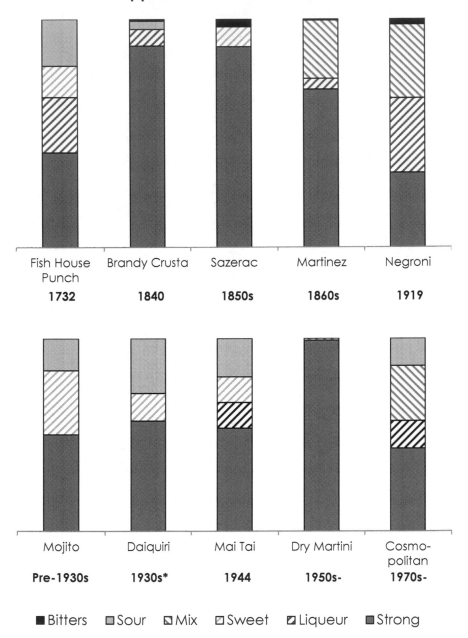

Fish House Punch	Brandy Crusta	Sazerac	Martinez	Negroni
1732	**1840**	**1850s**	**1860s**	**1919**

Mojito	Daiquiri	Mai Tai	Dry Martini	Cosmo-politan
Pre-1930s	**1930s***	**1944**	**1950s-**	**1970s-**

■ Bitters ▨ Sour ◪ Mix ▨ Sweet ▨ Liqueur ■ Strong

Notes

- By "mix" I mean an ingredient that contains significant parts sweet and sour. In this chart, "mix" applies to vermouth (both varieties) and cranberry juice.

- While each of these drinks can be found in the 1806 cocktail menu book, some of the recipe ratios are pulled from other sources. And for the history of each drink, I relied heavily on the work of the esteemed David Wondrich.

- The Negroni does not call for a concentrated bitters like Angostura or Peychaud's, but Campari contains a significant bitter component, so I've represented Campari here as an orange liqueur combined with bitters.

- *Though the Daiquiri is purported to have been invented in 1905, I've used the 1930s date here because Ernest Heminway popularized the drink in the late 1930s.

- Similarly, the dry martini has existed in theory since the first martini came about in the 1900s, but Google Ngram viewer proves the dry martini did not become popular until the 50s, peaking around the 80s.

But what does this really tell us? First off, It's easy to look at two drinks with similar formulas and see those similarities. For example:

The Old-Fashioned	vs.	The Sazerac
2 oz. 100-proof Rye Whiskey	vs.	2 oz. 100-proof Rye Whiskey
1 Sugar Cube	vs.	1 Sugar Cube
2 dashes Angostura	vs.	2 dashes Peychaud's
		1 dash Angostura
		Absinthe rinse
Lemon Peel	vs.	Lemon Peel

Stir spirits with sugar and bitters. Aromatize with lemon peel and/or Absinthe. Contemplate.

But what happens when you start dealing with liqueurs vs. syrups vs. vermouths? Different types of citrus? I thought it was difficult to see much outside the obvious using the chart from the previous page, so on the following page I've recreated the chart, this time with each major ingredient "normalized":

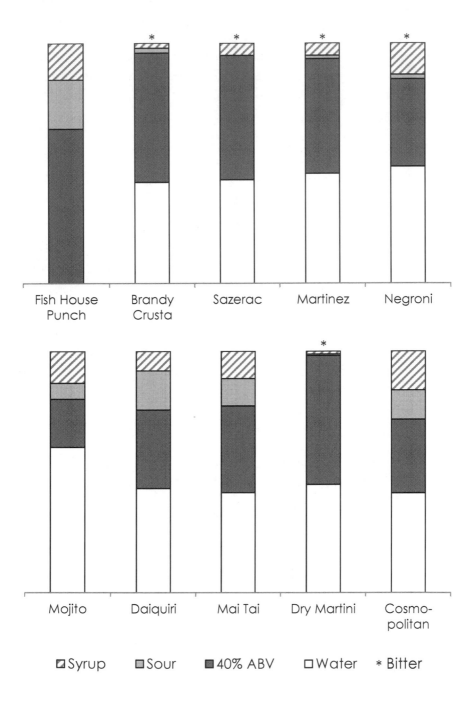

Notes

- In the preceding chart, I've estimated each drink's *equivalent* alcohol, water, simple syrup, and sour content. For ABV estimates, I used the the calculation methodology described at the end of the chapter "The Martini: In Pursuit of Perfect Balance."
- Alcohol is given in parts of 40% ABV spirits.
- Syrup is syrup given in parts of 1:1 simple syrup.
- Sour is given in parts of lemon juice equivalent.
- Water due to ice melt was estimated at 75% of original mass. The Mojito got an additional 75% due to the soda water content.
- I couldn't settle on an accurate way to quantify bitters (see "How Much is a Dash, Anyway?" In the chapter "Tasting, Sipping… Chugging Bitters"), so the notation merely points out whether the component exists.
- Here's an example of what I mean by equivalent. Consider vermouth, an ingredient present in the Martinez, Negroni, and Martini. Based on an ABV of 18%, an acidity of 3 pH, and a sugar content of roughly 10%, I estimated 1 part vermouth as equivalent to 0.44 parts spirits, 0.1 parts sour, 0.2 parts syrup, and 0.26 parts water.

The Vertical Approach: The Martinez, Over Time

For the visualizations shown in the first two charts of chapter, I used the following recipe for the Martinez cocktail: 2 oz. Gin, 0.75 oz. Sweet Vermouth, 0.25 oz. Maraschino liqueur, and 2 dashes of Angostura bitters.

But, if history is to be believed, the Martinez changed over time. As Eric Felten explains,[84] the Martinez was born of the classic Manhattan, but over time the Martinez turned into the classic Martini. As such, the Martinez makes a perfect candidate for some advanced visualization techniques.

---

[84] http://online.wsj.com/article/SB122912732510903205.html

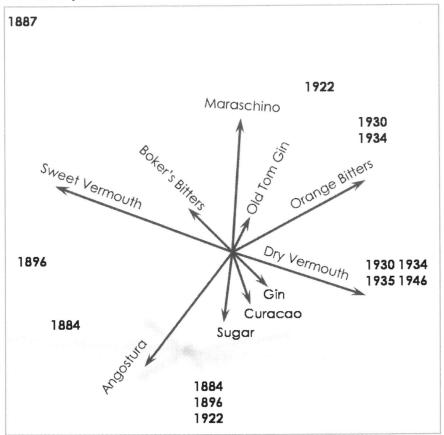

Arielle Johnson studies flavor chemistry and perception at the University of California, Davis. Her interests span the culinary map; when last we spoke, topics ranged from mass spectrometry of cocktail bitters to the microbiology of Miso, to the design of sensory booths for tasting sparkling wine.

The graph you see above is an example of what Arielle does in her spare time. It's called a **principle component analysis** and it visualizes how a given experimental sample differs from another, assuming that every sample has multiple variables associated with it. In our example, the samples are recipes for the Martinez cocktail, collected by bartender Tristan Stephensen of Purl and The Worship Street Worship Shop in London, UK. The variables are their ingredients, as labeled in the chart.

How do I read this thing?

Imagine graphing every possible ingredient in a Martinez. The task would require an axis for each variable; the graph would quickly bleed over into multiple dimensions. Principle component analysis uses linear algebra to collapse all of those dimensions down into 2-dimensional space, so it's easily readable. It also conveniently rotates all the data so that the most significant changes are shown along the x-axis and the second-most are shown along the y-axis. For more on reading PCAs, see the companion blog to this book. For simplicity's sake, I'll address the takeaways specific to this chart.

So, here's what you can gather from Arielle's graph:

- See how the vector for sweet vermouth points in the exact opposite direction as the one for dry vermouth? That means there are no drinks in which the two show up together.

- Note how Boker's, Angostura, and orange bitters point in 120° offsets from each other, but the vector for Boker's is shorter. This means that Boker's shows up less than the other bitters and the bitters are never combined.

- When two vectors point in orthogonal (perpendicular) directions, such as in the case of Maraschino and the vermouths, it means that the inclusion of one ingredient has no impact on whether the other will be included. That is to say, there are recipes that call for dry vermouth and Maraschino as well as recipes that call for sweet vermouth and Maraschino.

- Gin, curacao, and sugar point in similar directions; Old Tom Gin and Maraschino also point in similar directions. But the two groups point away from each other. This means there are multiple drinks that feature Old Tom and Maraschino and multiple drinks that include sugar, gin, and curacao, but none that feature the two groups together.

- Clusters of years indicate the formulas created in those years were similar in structure. Note how 1887 is off in a corner, by itself. This means that its formulation is very different from the others'.

- There are multiple entries for the years 1884, 1896, 1922, 1930, and 1934. And most of the duplicates do not appear near each other on the graph. This means that two drinks, both called "Martinez," were created in that year, and they were different from one another.

What does this all mean?

I hope the graphs in this chapter demonstrate how widely cocktail formulas can vary, both across drinks and even within a single drink.

Think of cocktails like dishes at a restaurant: if you order spaghetti and meatballs at a restaurant, you have a rough idea of what you'll get, but some variance is acceptable. Vary too far from the template and satisfaction plummets. For example—

When is an Old-Fashioned Not an Old-Fashioned?

Jeffery Morgenthaler explains:

In my bar [Clyde Common, in Portland, Oregon], if you order an old-fashioned, we make you an old-fashioned whiskey cocktail [whiskey, sugar, bitters]. But there is one place in the world where that shit don't fly.

Case in point: Clyde Common is located in a hotel, so we get a lot of travelers. One day, a guest was at the bar and ordered a brandy old-fashioned and so one of my bartenders served up a very nice drink—good cognac, bitters, sugar, and orange twist.

This lady, a traveler, just stared at the drink with this horrified expression on her face, as if the cocktail were some sort of dead animal. So I immediately swooped over there, snatched up the drink, and asked her "so, what part of Wisconsin are you from," to which she answered, "Madison."

You see, for five years or so, we actually made brandy old-fashioned's the way this lady liked them at the bar—with a cherry and an orange slice, muddled. But then people got all snooty about that and so we changed it back to the booze-sugar-bitters variant. But that version's like blasphemy in Wisconsin—the muddled brandy old-fashioned is practically the state drink of Wisconsin, and you can't forget stuff like that.

The Martini: In Pursuit of Perfect Balance

Look at this section not as a definitive guide to a perfectly balanced cocktail, but as a systematic way to set up an experiment and ask your own questions. Drinking 10 cocktails at once? All in the name of science.

The following experiment and writeup are by Australian bartenders Andrew Cameron and Angus Burton.

Enter Andrew and Angus

We've already met Andrew Cameron, microbiologist and bartender. Angus Burton was his partner in crime at Canvas Club before moving out to Melbourne, Australia in mid-2012. The below experiment was done when the pair were still working together at Canvas Club.

As scientists and bartenders, we must cater to each customer's preference when we make him a martini. We cannot control his choice of gin or vermouth or his ideal flavor profile.

But if we know about dilution and temperature and ratios, perhaps the application of this knowledge can help us to accurately suggest an ideal ratio of Gin to Vermouth, tweaked based on the brand of each ingredient.

Think of it as a "curve of palatability" along which delicious drinks may be found, where:

x = temperature

y = ABV of a liquid

We think it's important to keep in mind that given a physical space—a bar, for example—a process will consistently produce stirred cocktails at an identical temperature. That same recipe will then need to be tweaked when dealing with a different ambient temperature and humidity.

Experiment Setup

- We designed 10 martinis to be made in different proportions with different ABVs.
- The martinis would be tested by 4 judges, three of whom tasted blind. The fourth was making and tasting.
- We used a fresh bottle of Dolin Dry Vermouth.
- 7 experiments were conducted with Bombay Sapphire gin, at 40% ABV.
- 3 experiments were conducted with Plymouth Gin at 42.1% ABV

Results:

Test #	Gin Type	Gin (mL)	Vermouth (mL)	End Water (mL)	Temp (C)	Average Score (5=best)
1	Plymouth	60	30	40	2	3.5
2	Plymouth	60	10	35	3	2.25
3	Plymouth	60	20	40	-4	2.5
4	Bombay	60	30	110	2	1.75
5	Bombay	60	10	90	0	3
6	Bombay	60	30	50	5	2.5
7	Bombay	60	10	70	0	3.75
8	Bombay	60	20	55	0	3
9	Bombay	60	20	52	-2	2.5
10	Bombay	60	20	58	2	2.75

And the winners are:

Two Taste-Tested Martinis

60 mL Bombay Sapphire   -or-   60 mL Plymouth Gin
10 mL Dolin Dry Vermouth   -or-   30 mL Dolin Dry Vermouth

Stir well with ice, strain into a chilled cocktail glass. Do not garnish, lest you invite more variables to the party.

One small problem…

I applaud the labor that Andrew and Angus took to craft their ideal Martinis, but their experiment suffered from a flaw that plagues many cocktail geeks' understanding of dilution.

Basically, when alcohol is mixed with water, the volume of the result will be… weird. I'll show you what I mean in the next section, but I have to warn you: this is probably the most complex information in this book. Feel free to skip it if you're not interested.

How to Calculate the Final Temperature and ABV of a Cocktail

In this section, I give you the formulas you would need to calculate a drink's end dilution and temperature. But first, a disclaimer: **they don't work.**

That's right—the calculations for *final* temperature and dilution presented here will not be accurate because I simply couldn't account for all the complexities associated with mixing ethanol, water, and ice. The specifics of why are discussed in the body of the math. But here's why the calculations are still important: because (1) they show how to accurately calculate a drink's *starting*[85] alcohol content and water content, and (2) they give you some basic and useful understanding of how alcohol content, ice, and temperature interrelate in a cocktail.

Don't worry, this section is not entirely theoretical. Skip the math and go straight to the experimental results at the end for some concrete measurements and rules of thumb you can use on a daily basis. Read on for some fun calculations. First off,—

Temperature depends on dilution.

Ice mixed with water is known as a frigorific mixture. This means that as long as both components are present, the temperature of the mixture will always move toward equilibrium. In the case of ice and water, that equilibrium temperature is the freezing point of water, 32°F.

---

[85] Before stirring or shaking with ice, that is.

Add ethanol to the equation and an equilibrium temperature still exists, but it will be lower than the freezing point of water. Here are the numbers (ignore the mass fraction column for now, more on that later):

ABV	Mass Fraction	T_{Eq}		ABV	Mass Fraction	T_{Eq}
0%	0%	0°C		50%	44%	-32°C
10%	8%	-4°C		60%	54%	-37°C
20%	16%	-9°C		70%	65%	-48°C
30%	25%	-15°C		80%	76%	-59°C
40%	34%	-23°C		90%	88%	-73°C

When you shake a drink, the liquid contents will cool rapidly down to the equilibrium temperature, represented above as T_{Eq}. No matter how much more you shake the drink, it cannot get any colder than the equilibrium temperature.

What does this mean? As long as you know the starting ABV of a drink, it's easy to calculate its final temperature. Or is it? Here's the problem: as ice melts, it changes the ABV of a drink, which then changes the T_{Eq}. But, before we look at how to deal with this problem mathematically, we have to stop thinking in terms of ABV.

For calculations, use mass.

Although we usually talk about ethanol and water mixtures in terms of ABV, it's actually more useful for calculation purposes to talk about the *mass fraction* or *mass ratio*, a value that compares the mass of ethanol to the mass of water in a mixture.

Here's why: while mass always stays the same, ethanol and water do weird things when they mix and the density of an ethanol-water mixture will not correlate directly to the amount of either component in the mixture. Since ABV depends on volume, which depends on density, doing any sort of temperature or dilution calculations with ABV would be extremely difficult. The following chart shows the weird relationship between mass and ABV:

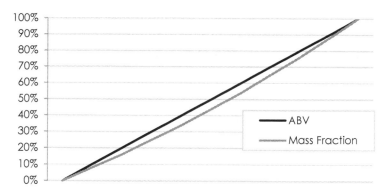

If we're going to solve for temperature and dilution given the starting masses of water and ethanol, we have to establish a relationship between mass and equilibrium temperature. If we plot mass against temperature, we can use a polynomial regression to establish that relationship:

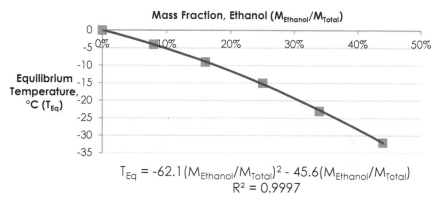

$$T_{Eq} = -62.1(M_{Ethanol}/M_{Total})^2 - 45.6(M_{Ethanol}/M_{Total})$$
$$R^2 = 0.9997$$

Notes

- Keep in mind that the above is not an equation, just a correlation between freezing temperature and mass fraction. That's why the units don't necessarily match up.
- I've only fit the regression to data up to 45% ABV because you'll almost never make a cocktail that starts outs with a higher ABV.

Time for some math.

Calculating the end dilution and temperature of a drink requires solving a system of equations, so I think it's easiest if I use a simple example. Let's analyze a 3:2:1 sour.

Calculation Sour

45 mL x 40% alcohol
30 mL Simple Syrup
15mL Lime Juice
Plenty of Ice

Directions to follow.

For the example, we'll treat simple syrup as if it were just water to make things simpler. To find the ethanol contribution of 40% ABV alcohol, we would first realize that 40% ABV corresponds to 34% mass fraction and then use the handy chart here[86] to find out that the density of a 34% ethanol and water mixture by weight is 0.947 kg/L.

Multiply 45 mL by 0.947 kg/L by 34% and you get 14.49 g ethanol. The following chart lists all the important numbers.

	Ethanol Content	Water Content
45 mL 40% Alcohol	14.49 g	28.13 g
30 mL simple syrup	0 g	30 g
15 mL lime juice	0 g	15 g
Total mass	14.49 g	73.13 g
Total mass fraction	16.5%	-
Total ABV	~20%	-

All of these numbers are the *initial* values for water and ethanol. What we want to solve for are the *final* values, which take into consideration the melting of ice.

The key unknown: ice melt.

Next, we set up our system of equations. The vast majority of heat transfer from ice into a drink comes from the *heat of fusion*, or the energy required to melt a gram of

---

[86] http://www.handymath.com/cgi-bin/ethanolwater3.cgi

ice into liquid water. It takes 1 calorie to raise the temperature of a gram of water one degree, but it takes 80 calories to melt a single gram of ice.

So, how many grams of ice will be needed to cool our drink down as cold as possible? Basically, one-eightieth the amount of drink you're cooling, multiplied by the change in temperature.

$$M_{Melted\ Ice} = (T_i - T_f) * M_{Drink}/80$$

Note that T_f is equal to T_{Eq}.

Assuming our ingredients start off at 20°C, we can combine the melted ice equation with the polynomial regression equation into something like this:

$$T_f = T_i - 80 * M_{Melted\ Ice}/M_{Drink}$$
$$T_f = -62.1(M_{Ethanol}/M_{Total})^2 - 45.6(M_{Ethanol}/M_{Total})$$

Since we know the starting mass of ethanol in the drink is 14.49g, the total mass of the drink is 87.62 grams, the starting temperature is 20°C, and the M_{Total} in this case is equal to $M_{Drink} + M_{Melted\ Ice}$, we substitute to get:

$$T_f = 20°C - 80 * M_{Melted\ Ice}/87.62g$$
$$T_f = -62.1 * (14.49/(87.62g + M_{Melted\ Ice}))^2$$
$$- 45.6(14.49/(87.62g + M_{Melted\ Ice}))$$

Toss these into an equation solver, like the online service Wolfram|Alpha, and we find that about 29 g of ice should melt to make a dilution of about 17% ABV and the final temperature should be about -6.6°C.

Sounds good, so why doesn't this work?
Because I did not account for the fact that **the mixing of ethanol and water is exothermic**, which means that when you mix ethanol and water, heat is released and that heat increases both ice melt (dilution) and final equilibrium temperature.

It's not like I'm just being lazy; there's no equation that neatly sums up the relationship between enthalpy (heat release), alcohol mass fraction, and water. Take a look at this paper[87] for a chart of the experimental data that shows the relationship.

Experimental data:

Of course, while all the above calculations are useful in theory, nothing beats experimental data. The following chart was the result of three runs using the same bottle of 190° Everclear. The lower-ABV tests were run with the Everclear diluted with filtered water. Drinks were shaken using a pre-chilled metal Boston shaker and glass top. All drinks were consumed shortly after experimentation (ouch).

Volumes were measured with a 100mL graduated cylinder, temperatures with a dual infrared/probe kitchen thermometer, and mass with an OXO kitchen scale. Starting temperature for all runs was approximately 71°F/22°C.

	Initial Volume, Mass	Final Temperature	Final Mass, ABV
95% Alcohol	60mL, 47g	15°F/-9.4°C	94g, 50%
75% Alcohol	60mL, 54g	21°F/-6.1°C	116g, 40%
40% Alcohol	60mL, 55g	24°F/-4.4°C	105g, 22%
20% Alcohol	60mL, 56g	26.5°F/-3.1°C	91g, 12%
Water	60mL, 60g	32°F/0°C	81g, 0%

Note:

- Note that alcohol is lighter than water, hence the difference between starting volume and starting mass. As noted previously in the discussion about ABV vs. mass fraction, the volume behaves strangely for other reasons as well. Look up "azeotrope" if you're curious.

- Note how the 95% alcohol ends up at 50% ABV and a final temperature of -9.4°C, well above the theoretical equilibrium temperature of -32°C. Why is this? I have no idea. I would love to find out more if someone out there can point me in the right direction.

---

[87] http://pubs.acs.org/doi/abs/10.1021/je60034a008 The chart's on the first page and the first page is free to access.

The "Perfect" Temperature and Dilution: Do They Exist?

In a word, no. After all the charts and visualizations of the previous two chapters, that's the only conclusion I can come to.

In my tests, the range of classic cocktail formulations looks something like this: At the low end, the Gin and Tonic has an ABV of about 10% at a temperature of between 32°F and 40°F. At the high end, the Old-Fashioned clocks in at about 25% alcohol and several degrees below freezing, depending on stirring time.

And there are other confounding variables. Our perception of acidity is related to pH, sure, but how sour a liquid tastes depends also on the type of acids present and the concentration of masking tastes like sugar and salt. Just look at the charts in "Old-Fashioned vs. Sazerac vs. Martinez" and see how acid levels vary between drinks.

Think about cocktail-making like cooking: there is set of boundaries within which you have to work, but as long as you stay in those boundaries, your options are limitless.

Then again, armed with some of the analytical tools I've laid out in these chapters, you can start thinking about drinks that push the boundaries. Let's look at one example in the next chapter.

The Manhattan and Hyperdilution

Let's start with an example to illustrate what I mean by "hyperdilution." Compare:

The traditional Manhattan:

Manhattan

2 oz. Rye Whiskey
1 oz. Sweet Vermouth
Two dashes Angostura Bitters

Stir with ice. Strain into chilled coupe glass. Garnish with three brandied cherries.

The "watered-down" Manhattan:

Strongwater
Courtesy Pip Hanson, Marvel Bar, Minneapolis, MN

180mL Water
30mL Booker's Bourbon
30mL Landy VS Cognac
10mL Carpano Antica Formula Vermouth
10mL Farigoule Thyme Liqueur
10mL Lemon Zest Syrup*

Build on the purest ice possible in the order given. Stir well.
Serve in a large (20-oz. ish) glass.

Note:

- the easiest way to make lemon zest syrup is to just crush the zest of 12 lemons into a cup of sugar, let sit for 45 minutes, then add half a cup of water and simmer until all the sugar is melted. This is basically an Oleo Saccharum.[88]

---

[88] See Jefferey Morgenthaler's post on the topic:
http://www.jeffreymorgenthaler.com/2012/vacuum-seal-oleo-saccharum/

The traditional Manhattan will chill down to a temperature of about 28°F, a few degrees below freezing. The Strongwater should be closer to 40°F. If, at first, you think an over diluted, warmer-than-normal Manhattan sounds terrible, consider this chart:

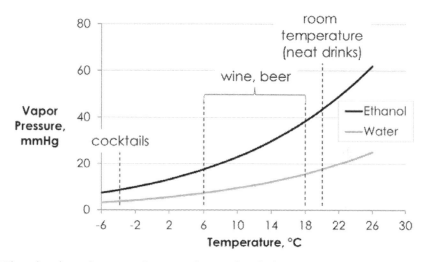

What the chart shows is what wine lovers already know: serve a wine too cold and it loses all of its aroma. The vapor pressure of a liquid correlates to how much of that liquid turns into a gas and floats above the glass. Since cocktails are a mixture of water and ethanol, the overall vapor pressure of a drink will lie somewhere between the two lines, depending on ABV.

Shaken cocktails are regularly served below 0°C, where vapor pressure is very low. This is one reason why it's so important to amplify aromas using citrus peels or aromatic spritzers. By diluting the Manhattan and serving it warmer, more of the aromas already present in the spirits are able to volatize and shine through.

As it would turn out, vapor pressure is only one part of the puzzle. Harold McGee explains:

> "Aroma molecules are also more chemically similar to alcohol molecules than they are to water, so they tend to cling to alcohol, and are quicker to evaporate out of a drink when there's less alcohol to cling to.

Here are some more examples.

Gatsby
Courtesy Pip Hanson, Marvel Bar, Minneapolis, MN

50mL Oban 14-year-old Scotch whisky
10mL Orchard Apricot
10mL Benedictine
12 drops Saline Solution (3 water : 1 salt)
80mL chilled Distilled Water

Serve all ingredients in a Riedel burgundy glass.

Ladykiller
Courtesy Pip Hanson, Marvel Bar, Minneapolis, MN

40mL Barley Shochu (Araki or other)
30mL Beefeater Gin
15mL Orchard Apricot liqueur
10mL Noilly Prat Dry Vermouth
10mL Lemon Zest Syrup
40mL Rose Wine
120mL chilled Distilled Water

As with the Strongwater, build on large pieces of the purest ice possible.

Pip says:

- This is a sort of "summer Strongwater" and is extremely popular. Interestingly, it is a great drink for the vodka water/vodka soda set, as they are really just

---

[89] http://www.nytimes.com/2010/07/28/dining/28curious.html

looking for a light, clean flavor. This drink is light, but full of subtle complexity at the same time.

We met Australian bartender Angus Burton in the previous chapter. He was kind enough to share two recipes with me for this chapter. First, an example of how easy it is to change ingredients around once you understand basic ratios.

Manhattan, Updated
Created by Angus Burton at Moon Under Water, Melbourne, Australia

30 ml Bulleit Rye Whiskey
30 ml Chopin Potato Vodka
30 ml Marsala
Dash of Angostura Bitters
Orange Twist

Stir with ice. Strain into chilled coupe glass. Express the orange twist, then discard.

Angus says:
- I was consulting for a restaurant where I was asked to produce 'classic' drinks. Not wanting to serve a boozy Manhattan as an 'aperitif' for a meal of delicate and extremely refined flavours, I made the drink with Chopin potato vodka, which has a smooth and creamy mouthfeel.

Next comes Angus' take on the hyperdiluted Manhattan. This drink takes the concept one step further than the other diluted examples in this chapter, as this cocktail is designed to be served at room temperature.

The MacNicol
Created by Angus Burton at Byblos, Melbourne, Australia

45ml Talisker Scotch Whisky
15ml Noilly Pratt Dry Vermouth
7.5ml Maraska Apricot Liqueur
7.5ml Mozart Dry Chocolate Liquor
5ml Rosso Antico

Stir down with ice and finish with an orange zest (discarded)

Note:

- As written, this recipe produces a standard stirred cold drink. But, when Angus first made it, he accidentally let it go to room temperature and realized it tasted even better warm than cold. To make the drink as a room-temperature cocktail, use 80 mL good-tasting water and skip the stirring with ice.

Angus says:

- The first time I made a drink that tasted better at room temperature than when it was freshly stirred on ice was a revelation to me and my workmates at the time. This drink was singled out as the stand-out signature cocktail at the World Class Australia Finals in 2011.

- The MacNicol is a peculiar drink in that it is 'brand-specific' in terms of its ingredients. I've made the drink 100 times with different whiskies, liqueurs and vermouths, and while I will never serve a drink I'm unhappy with, it's fair to say that the drink is at its best as originally (fortuitously) made.

For a review of the MacNicol with tasting notes, see the site
http://everydaydrinking.wordpress.com/2011/06/17/the-macnicol/

The Flip: Emulsions, With and Without Eggs

The flip began as a heated mixture of beer, rum, sugar, and spices.[90] Sailors would stab a red-hot poker into a barrel of these ingredients; the heat created nutty flavors, warmed everything, and foamed the beer and the foam gave the drink a slightly smooth mouthfeel.

At some point, bartenders started using eggs to recreate the silky mouthfeel of traditionally-made flips (I guess a red-hot poker was just too much work for them). Today, a flip is any drink that contains a whole egg, usually served cold, but sometimes hot, generally sweet and spiced in taste. Think of eggnog as the flip's close but heavier cousin.

Why eggs?
At its heart, a flip is an emulsion and all stable emulsions need three things:
1. A dispersed phase
2. A continuous phase
3. An emulsifier

Consider a vinaigrette made with only oil and vinegar. Shake, stir, or blend the two liquids together long enough and a creamy emulsion will result. But as soon as you stop applying force to the mixture, the oil will begin to separate from the vinegar. This is because vinegar (water) is polar, while oil is nonpolar.

Which phase is continuous and which dispersed depends on a number of factors, but is not defined simply by what material there is more of. Consider whipped cream. Heavy cream begins as an oil-in-water emulsion. As you whip it, it becomes an oil-and-air-in-water emulsion, and eventually it turns into butter, a water-in-oil emulsion.

---

[90] If Wikipedia and this Difford's Guide article are to be believed, that is:
http://www.diffordsguide.com/class-magazine/read-online/en/2011-09-27/page-8/what-the-flip

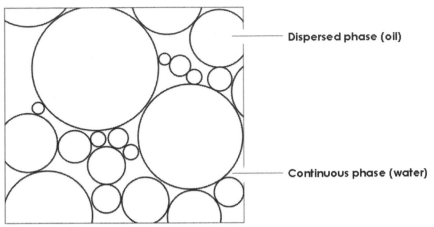

Dispersed phase (oil)

Continuous phase (water)

In cocktails, the continuous phase is always water. Ethanol is more soluble in water than it is in oil, so for our purposes it can be considered part of the continuous phase as well.

Eggs contain both nonpolar fat and polar water. Both egg whites and egg yolks contain a complex collection of amino acids that bond to both oil and water. Egg yolks also contain lecithin. Lecithin molecules have both a polar and a nonpolar end. Here's the takeaway: the stuff in egg whites and egg yolks all acts as emulsifiers, but egg yolks are stronger emulsifiers than egg whites.

Two techniques for separating egg yolks from egg whites: with the shells (left) and with your hands (right).

Why are Emulsions "Creamy"?

The mouthfeel of emulsions can get very complicated. The general rule: the smaller the particle size of the dispersed phase, the creamier the mouthfeel. Viscosity also matters. The end viscosity of an emulsion depends on the viscosities of both the dispersed and continuous phases, the strength of the emulsifier, and the particle size of the dispersed phase.

Not making sense? Let's look at a tasty example:

Absinthe Suissesse
Adapted from kindredcocktails.com

1.25 oz. Absinthe
½ oz. Homemade Orgeat
2 oz. Milk
1 Whole Egg
2 drops Orange Flower Water
3 drops Taza Chocolate Mexicano Extract

Combine first 4 ingredients. Shake with ice like a drunken monkey. Strain into a 6-oz. highball glass. Top with last two ingredients.

Notes:
- A simple recipe for orgeat can be found in the "Tiki Drinks" chapter.

In the above drink, the egg yolk contributes oil, which has a creamy mouthfeel. But emulsified air also imparts creaminess, and in this case, it makes up considerably more of the equation. To take this concept to its theoretical limit, I poured a complete Absinthe Suissesse into an ISI whipper and charged with N_2O cartridges. Result? The normally 7-oz. drink transformed into 20 fluid ounces of boozy, creamy, and delicious foam.

The creaminess of a foam depends on the size of its suspended air bubbles. Likewise, the creaminess of an oil-in-water emulsion depends on the bubble size of the oil. It doesn't so much matter what that oil happens to be. In traditional flips, egg yolks contribute the oil component. But, while egg yolk is delicious, bartenders can improvise by using alternative oils, as long as there are enough other emulsifiers in a drink to keep everything together. Here's an example:

Oliveto
Coutesy Pip Hanson, Marvel Bar, Minneapolis, MN

60 ml Gin
30 ml Lemon Juice
10 ml 2:1 Invert Syrup
10 ml Licor 43
1 Egg White
15 ml Olive Oil (California Olive Ranch sustainable extra virgin)

Preshake, shake again with ice, strain.

Notes:
- Pip says: "The olive oil brings an almost malic acid quality to this cocktail. It tastes fruity, like an apple or kiwi. If made correctly, this cocktail will not separate for a long time—much longer than the drink usually lasts. A quick stir with a spoon will re-emulsify the drink again, if it does begin to separate."
- Invert syrup describes syrup made with fructose and glucose instead of sucrose. Use the hot method for making syrup to approximate the thinner texture of invert syrup.
- Licor 43 is a complex Spanish herbal liqueur. Try Benedictine plus a drop of vanilla extract in its absence.

Don't all oils taste the same?
No. Most cooking oils (peanut oil, canola oil, etc.) taste the same because cooking oils are meant to cook food without imparting unwanted flavors. True extra virgin olive oils taste strongly of pepper, acidity, and floral notes, among other tastes, but they are relatively hard to find in the United States.

To taste a clearly strong-tasting oil, pick up a bottle of dark sesame oil from an Asian grocery and observe how nutty it smells. In this next drink, the toasted qualities of walnut oil are put into balance by lime juice and bright pisco.

Roasty Toasty
Courtesy Stephen Shellenberger, Pomodoro, Brookline, MA

2 oz. Cesar Pisco "Italia"
1 oz. Lime Juice
8 g Sugar
.5 oz. Roasted Walnut Oil
1 Egg White
Bittermen's Mole Bitters

Preshake, shake again with ice, strain. Garnish the foam with a few dashes of the bitters.

Notes:

- Feel free to substitute light rum, lightly-aged cognac, or cachaça for the pisco.
- It's possible to toast some nut oils at home in a skillet to up their roasty toasty-ness. Alternatively, you can roast roughly half a cup of walnuts in the oven at 350°F, then combine with a half cup plain old vegetable oil for a few hours to make a faux-toasted walnut oil.

What if you only use egg white and no oil at all?

Well, then you don't have a flip. But since you lose some richness by omitting the fat, egg-white-only drinks pair better with strong sours. Here's an example:

Fantastic Fizz
Created by Angus Burton at Canvas Club, Brisbane, Australia

25ml Laird's 7yo Apple Brandy
25ml LeBlon Cachaca
25ml St Germain Elderflower Liqueur
25ml Lemon Juice
20ml Egg White

Shake and strain into a fizz glass and top with soda
Finish with a lemon zest, discarded.

Is it Possible to Avoid Eggs Altogether?

Yes, but I would highly avoid against it. Egg white does two things well: it emulsifies oil into water and stabilizes a creamy head. If you're concerned about using raw eggs, powdered egg white makes a fine substitute. Use 2 tsp powder and 2 tbsp water for every egg white called for. Always hydrate egg white powder in warm water (never cold or hot). A stick blender helps.

If you're dealing with a customer who is allergic to eggs, I've found that a healthy dose of gum arabic (at least 1 part gum to 2 parts oil) will keep the oil emulsified. Add a small pinch of versawhip or methylcellulose to help stabilize a creamy head. See the chapter "The Cream Whipper: An Unlikely Multi-Tasker" for more ideas.

The Sour: Acid Alternatives to Citrus

The earliest cocktails were not boozy and bitter, as some might think. Actually, the ratios I used for the Fish House Punch, visualized in the chapter "Old-Fashioned vs. Sazerac vs. Martinez" most closely resemble the modern daiquiri, a traditional sour.

Modern bartenders are most familiar with citric acid because it's easily sourced from every citrus fruit (see more on citrus and acids in the chapter "Citrus: How to Maximize Aroma and Preserve Freshness). But that has not always been true. The below exploration of acids other than citric is adapted with permission from bartender and chemist Darcy O'Neill's phenomenal and eye-opening book *Fix the Pumps*. Emphasis is mine.

The History of Acids in Drinks

By Darcy O'Neill, author, Fix the Pumps, www.artofdrink.com

The use of **phosphoric acid** in cola beverages shouldn't be thought of as a true "phosphate". The reason cola based drinks still use phosphoric acid is that the flavour compliments the cola better than citric acid. The taste of phosphoric acid is described as astringent, dry and sharp in flavour while lacking the bright fruitiness of citric and **tartaric acids**. This is what made the phosphate class of drinks so interesting. The dry, astringent flavour must have worked well, otherwise they wouldn't have been popular for over 75 years.

It should be noted that acid phosphates are different than pure phosphoric acid because the phosphoric acid is mixed with the mineral salts of potassium, calcium, and magnesium. These salts are alkaline (basic pH) and when mixed with phosphoric acid react to create phosphate salts. This also neutralizes some of the phosphoric acid, making it less acidic.

The pH of the acid phosphate solution is between 1.7 and 2.0, or equivalent to that of fresh squeezed lime juice. In an 8 ounce glass of soda water; adding one teaspoon (5 ml) of acid phosphate gives the drink a pH of about 2.5, or the same as a can of cola.

The Avery Chemical Company introduced a new acid for aerated beverages in 1885, called "Lactart Acid of Milk". This was another proprietary composition, with the key ingredient being **lactic acid**. In the early 1900s, it was a very popular addition to soda fountain drinks.

Lactic acid is still widely used in the food and beverage industry. It has a mildly tart and agreeable flavor. It is naturally found in dairy products, but another example of its flavor would be Lambic and wheat style beers. The bacteria that ferment in these beers create lactic acid and give the beers their unique flavor.

The most common beverage acidifier today is **citric acid**. It is used in almost every soda pop—except the cola varieties—flavouring syrup and liqueur. It is a natural choice since it is commonly found in fruit.

Acids make an excellent medium for preserving foods, with vinegar (**acetic acid**) being well-known across time and cultures as a method of pickling foods. Vinegar was also a common drink for peasants in the middle ages, when beer was beyond their meagre means. American farmers were fond of a vinegar based beverage called Switchel (Haymaker's Punch). This drink was brought north by slaves in the West Indies, who called it "swizzle". The recipe is a simple combination of vinegar, a sweetener—usually molasses—and water.

Because vinegar was cheap and wasn't prone to spoiling like fruit acids, some proprietors used it in fountain drinks. However, beverage bottlers were condemned for its use in soda drinks, as the flavour was considered harsh.

Note:
- You can purchase acid phosphate and lactart on Darcy's blog, www.artofdrink.com

Drinking vinegar, you ask? Read more about them in the next section.

We want... a Shrubbery!!!

"First you must find... another shrubbery! Then, when you have found the shrubbery, you must place it here, beside this shrubbery, only slightly higher so you get a two layer effect with a little path running down the middle."

- Head Knight of Ni

In their modern iteration, shrubs are sour beverages allowed to ferment into vinegar, or simply syrups mixed with vinegar. The history of shrubs is as deep and rich as is the history of bitters. Whereas bitters began as indigenous medicines, shrubs were originally used to preserve fruit and mask the flavor of low-quality alcohol.

To this day, the term eludes definition. "Shrub" can refer to a type of sour syrup made with fresh fruit, a drink made with that syrup, or to a punch-like beverage made with fruit but containing no vinegar. It supposedly derives from the Arabic word "sharaba" (شرب), which means literally "to drink."[91]

For the purposes of this book, I will only address the version of "shrub" otherwise known as drinking vinegars, because that is how modern bartenders seemed to have adopted the term.

We've already met food blogger Carey Nershi (see "Drink to Convert the Cocktail Novice"). Her recent infatuation with drinks began with sodas, turned into an obsession with shrubs, and of course those shrubs made delicious cocktails. I'll let Carey take it from here.

Carey Nershi on Homemade Shrubs

Adapted from posts on Carey's blog, www.reclaimingprovincial.com
When you hear the phrase "drinking vinegar," what comes to mind? Weird old-timey medicine? Something gross you'd drink if you were doing some sort of "cleanse"? It's vinegar. And you drink it. That doesn't sound delicious at all.

---

[91] For more on the history of shrubs, see http://www.diffordsguide.com/class-magazine/read-online/en/2011-08-09/page-3/shrubbery

A shrub is a beverage made from fruit, sugar, and vinegar, which dates back to the days when preservation via refrigeration was not an option. Instead, people would macerate fruit and sugar together to extract the juices, then steep everything in vinegar for a week or so. Then they'd filter out the fruit, and be left with a delicious drinking vinegar.

Shrubs have made quite a comeback in recent years, and for good reason—they're awesome. Their sweet-yet-tangy flavor makes for a refreshing beverage when mixed with seltzer. And that same punchy taste can also do wonderful things in cocktails. And with a variety of fruits, sugars, and vinegars to mix and match, the combinations are nearly endless.

If you'd like to learn a little bit of history about shrubs, Serious Eats has a great article[92] that includes two different methods for making them (hot- and cold-processed).

For my shrubs, I followed the cold-processed method. Call me old fashioned, but I think there's something much more appealing and wholesome about giving the ingredients a few days to naturally get acquainted with one another, rather than tossing some stuff in hot sugar water and straining it out after a matter of minutes, then throwing in some vinegar and calling it a day. I can only speak to the results of the cold method, but what I can say about that is it only requires patience and stirring, and the end result is amazing. I already know that I will be making this many, many more times this summer.

---

[92] http://drinks.seriouseats.com/2011/06/cocktail-101-how-to-make-shrub-syrups.html

Strawberry Rhubarb Shrub Syrup
Recipe courtesy Carey Nershi, ReclaimingProvincial.com
Originally adapted from Fudge Ripple[93]
Yields about 2 cups of syrup

1 1/4 cups Ripe Strawberries, cleaned, hulled, and sliced
3/4 cup Rhubarb, cleaned and sliced
1 1/2 cups Granulated Sugar
10 Black Peppercorns, slightly crushed
1 cup Balsamic Vinegar
1/2 cup Cider Vinegar

Combine fruit, peppercorns, and sugar in a bowl or jar, stirring to evenly-coat the fruit. Cover and let sit for 24 hours at room temperature. Add the vinegars and stir well. Store the mixture at room temperature for 7–9 days, giving it a good stir each day. When finished, strain the mixture, then transfer to a clean jar or container. Store syrup in the fridge.

For a tasty cocktail, combine 1 part syrup with 1 part reposado Tequila and 2.5 parts carbonated water.

Notes:

- Using the cold-processed method keeps the volatile aromatics where they belong: in the syrup.
- The times given in this recipe worked for Carey, but your experience may vary. In my opinion, you should strain and move things to the fridge as soon as everything comes together and no more chunks of sugar remain. Leaving syrup out at room temperature—even acidified syrup—can lead to microbial growth.

---

[93] http://fudgeripple.blogspot.com

Plum-Orange Shrub Syrup
Recipe courtesy Carey Nershi, ReclaimingProvincial.com
Yields about 2 cups of syrup

2 cups Plums, pitted and chopped
zest of 1 Orange
10 Black Peppercorns, slightly crushed
2 cups Light Brown Sugar
1 1/2 cups Cider Vinegar
1/2 cup Balsamic Vinegar

Use the same procedures as described for Strawberry-Rhubarb Shrub, preceding.

For a tasty cocktail, combine 1 part applejack, 1 part syrup, ½ part rye, 2.5 parts ginger ale or ginger beer, and a few dashes of apple bitters, the recipe for which can be found on reclaimingprovincial.com

And now for something completely different. ^_^

Playing with Acid Powders

Today, it's easy to cheaply purchase small amounts of different acids to play around with in drinks. My notes on a few are below:

- **Citric acid.** Tastes just like the outside of a sour gummy. Most notably, it produces a back-of-the-mouth salivation that makes me want to describe the acid as "juicy."

- **Lactic acid.** Kind of chemically. After dissolving in water, it measured the same pH as the other acids, but I thought it tasted slightly less sour. I didn't pick up on any dairy notes, but I also haven't tried this in a cocktail. Much more powdery and less soluble than the other acids.

- **Malic acid.** Really fun and exciting to play with. There was a noticeable tingle on the tongue from this acid that reminded me of biting into a tart apple.

- **Tartaric acid.** I was expecting this to taste like "grape" but the word I wrote down was "clean." Very similar to citric acid, with perhaps just slightly less "juiciness."

What are concentrated acids used for?

In modernist cooking, the acids listed above are usually used as acidity regulators—that is, to decrease the pH of a dish so that a chemical process either occurs or is prevented. In mixing drinks, these acids can be used to precisely adjust the acidity of a drink without introducing citrus flavors or cloudiness from fruit particulates.

Practical Application

At Booker & Dax bar in New York City, NY, Dave Arnold serves up amazing cocktails held up with a backbone of modern technique. In the Chartruth, he combines Green Chartreuse with agar agar-clarified lime juice. Here's my riff on the drink, using what we know about acids as a guide.

Carbonated Chartreuse Sour
Inspired by Dave Arnold, CookingIssues.com

1.5 oz Green Chartreuse
1 g Citric Acid
0.5 g Malic Acid
5 oz. Water
Lime Extract

Combine first 4 ingredients and 3 drops lime extract and let chill overnight. Carbonate and serve in a chilled highball glass. Garnish with two spritzes of lime extract.

Notes:

- Some useful data for you: 1.44 g/oz. vs. 1.38 g/oz. titratable (total) citric acid in lemon juice vs. lime juice.[94]
- It works best to carbonate this drink in batches of at least 2 so it fills up the SodaStream more completely.
- To make your own lime extract, add 1 drop lime essential oil to 1 oz. vodka.

---

[94] Penniston et al, *Quantitative assessment of citric acid in lemon juice, lime juice, and commercially-available fruit juice products (2008)*.

And what about a sour that contains no fruit juice?

Martini Sour
Inspired by Stephen Shellenberger, Pomodoro, Brookline, MA

2 oz. Gin
1 oz. Dry Vermouth
1 oz. 1:1 Simple Syrup
1 g Tartaric Acid Powder
Scant pinch Wine Tannin (optional)

Combine all ingredients at room temperature, stir to dissolve the acid. Once the acid is dissolved, stir with ice and strain into a chilled coup glass. Garnish with an orange or lemon peel, discarded.

Notes:

- As far as I know, no one has ever tried making a drink like this, except for Stephen Shellenberger, who tried it back in 2008 with a Batavia Arrack-based drink. What I did was increase the pH of the dry vermouth until it got to around the acidity of lemon or lime juice (2.3 ish pH) and then mixed a standard 4:2:1 daiquiri ratio. I then added simple syrup until the drink tasted more "neutral" as a result of mutual taste suppression.

- The drink ended up tasting clean and refreshing, and the herbal notes of the gin and vermouth easily shine through. At the same time, the added sweetness and acidity give this "martini" more body in the mouthfeel than you're used to. It's a very cool effect, and I'd love to see other riffs on this idea.

- I really liked the wine tannin in this drink: it helps to thin out the mouthfeel added by the simple syrup. I call for a scant pinch because the amount used it was even less than even my jewelry scale could measure. Wine tannin is available very cheaply online through homebrewing supply stores.

Tiki Drinks: To Future Adventures in Mixing

I end this book with a brief look at tiki drinks for two reasons:

1. I wish I knew more about tiki drinks.
2. "Tiki," like "craft," defines a state of mind, not a collection of recipes.

At first glance, tiki culture seems like the complete antithesis of craft cocktail culture. Tiki drinks were not sipped in dark and hidden speakeasies, they were chugged in bright faux-polynesian restaurants gaudily advertised by neon signs. And I would be happy to dismiss tiki in its entirety, if it were not for one simple incongruous fact: tiki drinks, properly made, taste *amazing*.

Below are a few short explorations of some extremely basic tiki drinks. For much, much more, I encourage you to take at some of the links and books linked on the companion blog to this book. Maybe I'll bump into you on one of those sites.

The Mai Tai and an Easy/Blasphemous Take on Orgeat

When did the Mai Tai become a Chinese restaurant staple? In Chinese, the words "mai tai" literally mean "to sell a desk." Delicious? After reading through a handful of eGullet and blog posts on the drink, I came to the conclusion that a proper Mai Tai requires three elements:

1. Good rum.
2. A proper balance between sweet and sour.
3. Tasty orgeat.

Here's my favorite recipe, based on many nights of trial and error. Many others exist; check out this post[95] for a whole spreadsheet full of combinations.

---

[95] http://rumdood.com/2009/01/26/a-month-of-mai-tais/

Mai Tai

*Inspired by Dushan Zaric, Employees Only, New York, NY
and Matt Robold, rumdood.com*

2 ounces Appleton Estate 12-year-old Rum
¾ ounce Marie Brizard Orange Curaçao
¾ ounce Orgeat
1 ounce Lime Juice

Shake and strain over fresh ice. Garnish with lime shell and a sprig of mint.

The above recipe calls for (1) a good rum and (2) a proper balance between sweet and sour. Now, onto the third element: orgeat (a French word pronounced or-Jah) began as a syrup made with barley, but the barley was eventually replaced with almonds. I will forego the history here and skip straight to the more important question: **what makes the best-tasting orgeat?**

Luckily, David J. Montgomery (perhaps better known as his online moniker *Professor Cocktail*) performed a taste test between eight different orgeat formulas, from coffee syrup to fancy concoctions sold in wine bottles. His favorites:

- **B.G. Reynolds Orgeat:** "rich, nutty, and delicious"
- **Small Hand Foods Orgeat:** "rich, balanced flavor and texture"

I hurriedly ordered a bottle of the B.G. Reynolds orgeat, but I couldn't find Jennifer Colliau's (owner of Small Hand Foods) orgeat anywhere. And that probably makes sense: she uses fresh almonds for each batch and has to rent space in a commercial kitchen to prepare all of her syrups by hand. It's hard to find her syrups on the East coast, as they're usually snatched up by local bartenders.[96]

---

[96] As of this writing, Jennifer has started an online store at http://smallhandfoods.com/ —here's hoping her products become more widely available!

The obvious question then becomes:

How could I imitate the best orgeat recipes at home?

I almost teared up with joy when I finally settled on my favorite orgeat recipe. I had been messing around with almonds for nearly a year, having thrown out gallons of terrible syrup, before I finally found one worth sharing.

The fact that the best-tasting orgeat I was able to create also happened to be the simplest was nothing short of beautiful:

Simply Awesome Orgeat
Yield: 1 Cup

184 g Pacific brand Almond Milk
88 g Sugar
8 drops (1/8 tsp) Almond Extract
4 drops (1/16 tsp) Orange Blossom Water

Combine ingredients.

Of course, a ton of testing and research went into the development of such a simple recipe. **Here are the highlights:**

- How does orgeat differ from almond syrup? Orgeat contains orange flower water and almond solids, while syrups use nothing more than almond flavoring (extract).

- Using normal almonds to make almond milk for orgeat actually doesn't do the flavor justice. Commercial almond milk is made with bitter almonds, which contain significantly more benzaldehyde—the key contributor to almond flavor. Unfortunately, bitter almonds can be poisonous when handled incorrectly. Why not just use good-quality extract that already contains benzaldehyde?

- Most homemade orgeat recipes call for blanching, steeping, or blending fresh almonds. As it would turn out, so do most almond milk recipes. Buying good-quality retail almond milk saves a tremendous amount of work while maintaining the critical fats and proteins of almond solids.

- Not all almond milks are created equal. Look for almond milk with minimal sodium and make sure one of the first ingredients listed is almonds. SO Delicious contains 90 mg sodium and 1 g of sugar.
- Do **not** heat the milk and sugar when combining. Heat will make the almond solids separate and also cause a foam to form.
- Almond solids quickly separate out of solution. Commercial almond milk contains thickeners and emulsifiers to keep the solids in solution. I preferred Pacific brand because it was the least viscous of the brands I tried, but any almond milk will work in a pinch.
- Most commercial almond milk contains a substantial amount of sodium. Keep in mind the suppressive effect this will have on finished drinks: adjust accordingly.
- Some almond milk brands contain more sugar than others. Make sure to adjust your sugar levels accordingly.

Improvise with Almost Instant Allspice Dram

Some things just make so much sense to make at home. And allspice liqueur is one of them. There are some ingredients that need to be macerated; the spices traditional to allspice dram don't. The oils and oleoresins in dried spices don't suffer at all from having the crap beaten out of them. For more on ideal infusion methods, see the chapter "For Every Particle, a Filter" and look under "How to Filter Anything" for more on this topic.

And yes, I have tested my formulation against the retail brands. I like mine better:

Almost-Instant Allspice Dram
Inspired by Chris Amirault, eGullet Forums

50g Allspice Berries (about 1/2 cup)
6 Black Peppercorns
10 Whole Cloves
1 Cinnamon Stick
1/2 a whole Nutmeg
225 mL Overproof (151-proof) Rum

300 g Sugar
300 g Water

Combine all ingredients except sugar and water in a blender. Blend on low for 5 minutes. Meanwhile, use the sugar and water to make 1:1 simple syrup. Remove the blended spices and rum from the blender and strain using the AeroPress® method or triple-layered cheesecloth. Combine with the simple syrup and you are DONE.

The Pina Colada and the Maillard Reaction

What does an ingredient like Allspice Dram do in a complex Tiki drink? It adds a deep, nutty note suggestive of baked Christmas cookies. I recommended 5 different spices in my Allspice Dram recipe, but what if I said many of those same flavors could be drawn from a single ingredient?

Remember the recipe for burnt sugar syrup in the chapter "Tinctures, Oils, and Extracts?" As it would turn out, caramelization is just one type of **browning reaction**; the other type is the **Maillard reaction**. The basic difference between the two? Think of caramelization as a carbohydrates-only party, while Maillard likes to hang out with proteins as well. Caramelization only requires sugars, such as sucrose, fructose, or glucose. With the Maillard reaction, amino acids (the building blocks of proteins) contribute nitrogen and sulfur atoms to the fun.[97]

The Maillard reaction will usually only occur at temperatures above the boiling point of water.[98] This means that it's not easy to brown liquids using the Maillard reaction without first evaporating most of the water content. That is, unless you use a pressure cooker. Pressure cookers typically maintain a pressure of 15 pounds per square inch, or PSI. At that pressure, water doesn't boil until it reaches 250°F/110°C—plenty hot enough for the Maillard reaction to occur.

Toasted Coconut Cream
Adapted from instructions by Laura Pazzaglia, HipPressureCooking.com

1 can Goya brand Cream of Coconut
Water

In a pressure cooking, fully submerge a can of Cream of Coconut on its side. Use a steamer basket or other utensil to ensure the can does not touch the sides of the cooker. Heat to 15 PSI and cook for 50 minutes.

Safety precautions: Allow the cooker to cool down naturally before you remove the can. Then, allow the can to cool down to room temperature before opening and using.

Notes:
- The sides and bottom of a pressure cooker can overheat, causing the Cream of Coconut to burn. That's why you don't want the can to touch the sides.
- The cool thing about this technique is that the Cream of Coconut will stay good as long as the any other canned good, so you can make it in batches.

---

[97] Listen to Harold McGee read his classic explanation of the Maillard Reaction live on the radio here: http://www.heritageradionetwork.com/episodes/3353-Cooking-Issues-Episode-106-Live-Readings-with-Harold-McGee

[98] For an excellent visualization that explains the Maillard reaction, see http://sciencefare.org/visualizations-science-concepts/

Toasted Coconut Colada

Inspired by Stephen Shellensberger, Pomodoro, Brookline, MA

For two drinks:
3 oz. Rum Agricole
1 oz. Madeira
2 oz. Toasted Coconut Cream
2 oz. Lime Juice
0.25 g Xanthan Gum (optional)

Add all ingredients and equal parts ice into a blender and blend on high until smooth.

Stephen Says:

- This might be my most successful attempt so far at trying to use a pressure cooker to augment aroma for the sake of a cocktail. The aroma really takes on a lovely quality reminiscent of so many desserts I've had featuring toasted coconut.

- The Cream of Coconut has to be blended after opening the can to re-homogenize all the fat. This can be done in a nice blender like a Vitamix or I use a colloid mill, though that is probably overkill. If it is homogenized well you won't get flecks of fat clinging to the sides of the glass at all.

My notes:

- I guess my blender just couldn't cut it—no matter what setting, I still couldn't get all the fat to emulsify. To avoid this problem, chill the toasted coconut cream in a shallow Tupperware container and simply skim the fat from the top.

- The xanthan gum helps the ice stay suspended in liquid, but don't bother if you don't have it. Also, the 0.25 grams called for is not exact—I usually just grab a tiny pinch with my fingers and mix it in.

Future Adventures and Parting Thoughts

Please think of this book as a work in a progress, a "v0.9" if you will. I'm choosing to release it at this stage because more than anything else, the techniques and ideas in this book need to be tested and there's no one better qualified to do that than the geeky folks who would be willing to shell out a few bucks to read this book. That would be you.

I look forward to learning from and arguing with you all in the coming months and years at the companion blog to this site. Perhaps we can even meet in person over a drink or two. I promise I'm much better looking when I'm in real life and when you're drunk.

When I set out to write this book, I thought I could cover all the important topics in cocktail innovation, but I couldn't have been more wrong. If I've learned anything through this year of writing, it is that: at its core, crafting a cocktail is no different from cooking. There will be new cocktails, new ratios, even entire new families of drinks—as long as there are creative bartenders willing to dream them up.

So think of this parting of ways not as the end of this book, but as the beginning of more explorations. And consider the following recipe as the first blog post that accompanies the book, if you will. It features many of the techniques discussed in this book—see if you recognize them. Tweet you later.

Elective Surgery

Created by Angus Burton at Canvas Bar, Brisbane, Australia

30 mL Appleton 8 Year Old Rum
15 mL Tanqueray Gin
10 mL Orgeat
10 mL Sake
10 mL Apricot Brandy
25 mL Lime Juice
45 mL Turmeric Soda (see below)

Shake and strain. Top with soda. Garnish with extravagant fruit.

Notes:

- Featured on The Best Cocktail List in Australia, as awarded by the 2012 Australian Bar Awards.

- To make turmeric syrup, heat 25 g (3 tbsp) turmeric powder with 1 L water, cool, strain, then add to 1 Kg sugar. When carbonating the syrup, use a ratio of 4 parts water to 1 part syrup.

Odds and Ends

Find the Cocktail Recipes You Really Want

Give a man a cocktail and he'll be happy for one night. Teach a man to mix and he'll enjoy every day of his life. If someone hasn't said this yet, they should. Ten years ago, the first modern books with craft cocktails were just hitting the shelves. Finding a great recipe was as simple as opening one of those books. Today, the database of possible cocktail recipes has swollen to include books, forums, blogs, and any number of other sources. Below are a few tricks for finding the diamonds in the rough.

On meta-searching. When I started getting interested in craft cocktails, I failed to take my own advice. Instead of choosing one or two drinks and buying only the bottles needed to create them, I resolved to taste every craft cocktail I could find. I downloaded the *Anvil 100 List*, or Anvil's "list of 100 cocktails you must try before you die," and started mixing.[99] Anvil's list is actually the bar's menu and cocktail menus make great starting points. Find the recipes you loved at a bar, then find them in the resources discussed below. For a list of curated cocktail menus, see Camper English's Alcademics blog.[100]

Cocktail Book Classics, Old and New

The Old: If you're looking to get serious about cocktail archaeology, start with *Imbibe!* By David Wondrich and *Vintage Spirits and Forgotten Cocktails* by Ted Haigh. Both books are available for preview through Google books. For an expansive list of vintage cocktail books, ordered by publication date, search for a Blogspot blog called <u>Vintage Cocktail Books</u>. A selection of some of those books are available free as PDFs through the website <u>Golden Age Bartending</u>. Stephen Shel-

---

[99] Anvil Bar and Refuge is an Austin, TX-based restaurant.
[100] http://www.alcademics.com

lenberger also maintains an ongoing project to share topical books about alcohol on his blog <u>Boston Apothecary</u>.

Modern Classics: Below are two lists of curated cocktail recipe books. The titles on the left are all the work of Gary Regan, a dude who was making craft cocktails before most modern bartenders were born. The latter three titles on the left are Regan's attempt to curate the recipes of the best bartenders working when the books were written.

The Vertical Approach	The Horizontal Approach
Joy of Mixology	The Craft of the Cocktail
New Craft Cocktails	Joy of Mixology
Annual Manual for Bartenders 2011	Art of the Bar
Gaz Regan's 101 New Best Cocktails 2012	Speakeasy
	PDT
	Drinks

The books on the right show how the same craft drink can be made in different ways. *Speakeasy* and *PDT* list the most classic cocktails while the relatively recent (and still not widely available in the U.S.) *Drinks* by Tony Conigliaro focuses on advanced techniques.

Convert Books into Searchable References

Cut the binding; scan the book. Some books are worth more to me as searchable pdf's than as paper and ink. For example: Gary Regan's *Joy of Mixology* is black and white, has few pictures, and contains pages of landscape-oriented charts.

The process is actually surprisingly simple. Take the books to a place that does printing services, like most office supply stores. Cutting a book binding costs something like $1/book. Scan the pages in using a home scanner. I use the Canon P-150. Run optical character recognition (OCR) on the resulting pdf's. I use Adobe Acrobat, recognize text, ClearScan at 600 dpi. If you don't have the right equipment or software, consider using a service like 1dollarscan.com, which charges $1/100 pages of a book.

At least digitize the index—no cutting required! If you can't bring yourself to cut a book binding or you're faced with a book that's larger than a standard scanner can handle, then at least digitize the index or table of contents. I did this with my copy of *Modernist Cuisine*. You'll need a decent camera, a tripod, good lighting, a cardboard box, duct tape, and a piece of plexiglass. After you take pictures of the index pages, run the jpg's through the program scantailor,[101] then OCR the text. There's tons more information on this process over at the DIY Bookscanner project.[102]

I keep a text document in Evernote with the text of the indexes of all the cocktail books that I own. <u>Eat Your Books</u> is a commercial website that does the same thing: it catalogs the recipe indexes of all kinds of cookbooks and allows you search them all at once, for a small monthly fee.

I have Tequila and Chartreuse—What Can I Make?

Filter the web. I am used to instant gratification. If I can't find a decent recipe in less than three minutes, I'm as likely as not to just start pouring shots. Let's assume you want to make something with Chartreuse and Tequila using only recipes found on gazregan.com. Here's the search syntax you'd use for Google:

```
site:gazregan.com amaretto and tequila
```

With this search you'd discover the "Foreword" by Nick Caputo.
And for a cocktail using gin and mint but not lemon, from either Alcademics or Kindred Cocktails, use the syntax:

```
site:alcademics.com OR site:kindredcocktails.com gin and mint -lemon
```

With that search, you'd find the "Gin-Gin Mule."

---

[101] http://scantailor.sourceforge.net/
[102] http://www.diybookscanner.org/

Maybe you don't care about the site and just need to use specific ingredients. Try:

```
Gin (lime OR lemon)
```

These simple search techniques also work on Google Books and within many blogs. For example, it's easier to search the recipes on Cocktail ~~Virgin~~ Slut using blogspot's built-in search engine than with the main Google search engine.

How do I find the great cocktail blogs? There are simply too many to list here and they are constantly changing. See the companion blog to this book for a current list. For one curated list, see Ted Haigh's recommendations in *Vintage Spirits and Forgotten Cocktails*. My favorite sites for recipes are Fred Yarm et al.'s <u>Cocktail ~~Virgin~~ Slut</u> and <u>Kindred Cocktails</u>. Also check out the forums at <u>eGullet</u> and <u>Chanticleer Society</u>.[103]

Here's another approach: to find the latest and greatest blogs, try searching for the blogs that *link* to the ones you already like. For example, the below search will return only blogs that reference Cooking Issues and also mention cocktails in the text:

```
link:cookingissues.com cocktails blog
```

Using this search, you might discover betacockails.com—a blog that's most certainly worth your visit.

A picture's worth a thousand words. As evidenced by the contributions from bloggers in this book, some great recipes can be found at food blogs and other non-cocktail-centric websites. To quickly find recipes from sites like these, simply search for a cocktail recipe or ingredient on Google images. Pictures from retailers and distributors will be plain-looking product placement shots. Scan for the images with interesting, personal backgrounds (like fruit, an accompanying dish, or someone's living room). These are most likely the work of talented food bloggers with a taste for good cocktails.

---

[103] <u>http://forums.egullet.org</u> | http://chanticleersociety.org/forums/

Permanent Aroma: Cocktail Bubbles

When people think "cocktails" and "science" they typically think spherification, liquid nitrogen, and molecular gastronomy. I've intentionally neglected these topics in this book because science is in every drink, not just those that rely on novelty for their appeal. Alton Brown may have put it best:

> "[on molecular gastronomy:]...all food is molecular and there is as much magic (and science) in a properly poached egg as there is in an edible paper pouch full of lavender smoke, powdered goat butter, and licorice caviar. With saffron foam no less.
>
> Some...such as myself would argue there is even more magic in that simple egg."[104]

With that being said, modern techniques can add a new dimension to flavor when wielded by the right hands. I follow dozens of "molecular" food blogs, but none of them compares to Molecular Recipes, a blog mixed with a storefront that posts recipes, interviews with chefs, and features incredible photos. They were kind enough to allow me to share this recipe with you:

---

[104] http://altonbrown.com/2011/08/upon-the-matter-of-molecular-gastronomy/

These cranberry bubbles are a great easy way to add a molecular gastronomy touch to the traditional cosmopolitan cocktail. The bubbles are made using the "bubbles with air pump" technique (see below).

There are several molecular gastronomy techniques that have been developed to incorporate air into liquids and creams to make them lighter. The two most popular are probably airs and foams. But now, get your fish tank air pump ready! The "bubbles with air pump" technique produces a result similar to "airs" but with larger bubbles. I believe this technique was developed by molecular gastronomy Chef Grant Achatz of Alinea in Chicago.

Airs are usually made by adding soy lecithin powder to a liquid and incorporating air using an immersion blender on the surface of the liquid. Foams are made by whipping or using an N_2O siphon such as the ISI Whip with a liquid with high fat content (cream), egg whites, versawhip or methylcellulose to name a few.

The "bubbles with air pump" technique consists of injecting air using a fish tank air pump into a liquid with some viscosity. It works great with light syrups and juices by just adding a little egg white powder and xanthan gum.

One of the advantages of this technique is that you can just leave the air pump running all the time so you always have bubbles ready to be served. Another interesting way of applying this technique is to fill the bubbles with smoke or herb, flower or spice vapor so the aromas are released when the bubbles burst.

If you don't have a fish tank air pump you could use for this, I recommend buying the inexpensive and silent Tetra Whisper Air Pump.

Cranberry Bubbles

380 g (13.4 oz) cranberry juice
1.5 g egg white powder
(or 1 g Versawhip)
1 g xanthan gum (buy xanthan gum)

Mix cranberry juice and egg white powder with immersion blender. Add the xanthan gum and mix again with immersion blender until completely dissolved.

Connect a clean PVC hose to a fish tank air pump and insert the other end in the mix. Turn the pump on and let bubbles collect for a few minutes. Collect some of the cranberry bubbles with a slotted spoon and place on top of your favorite Cosmopolitan recipe.

For more of Molecular Recipes' amazing work on mixed drinks, see http://www.molecularrecipes.com/molecular-mixology/molecular-mixology/

Does Hot Water Really Freeze Faster than Cold?

I'm including this short excerpt from ice expert Doug Shuntich for two reasons: (1) this is the best explanation of the "Mpemba effect"[105] I've seen and (2) it serves as a case study of some of the factors discussed in the earlier chapter on freezing clear ice.

Some people find that warm water or boiled water will freeze (i.e. Nucleate) faster than cooler water. This is sometimes true. Here is what is happening...

Start with 2 cups of water placed in the same freezer at 0°F. Initial conditions are: Cup A is hot at 120°F, Cup B is cool at 60°F. Both cups begin a rapid cooling process, but Cup A's cooling curve is much steeper due to the larger temperature differential.

Cup B will go through a relatively mild thermo "flipping" at 40°F (the temperature of maximum density). This flipping occurs when the coldest water at first sinks due to greater density, but later on floats as it becomes less dense than water at 40°F. The softer temperature gradient of Cup B means the water will be more 'stable' through this transition than the water in Cup A.

Cup B will subsequently go through the supercooling phase at 32°F in a more stable configuration than Cup A, resulting in 'deeper' supercooling temps prior to nucleation.

Finally, Cup A will likely nucleate, i.e. begin freezing, near 30-32°F due to its relative instability caused by rapid transitions through the 2 key phases mentioned above, while Cup B remains in supercooled liquid form even at 25°F or lower. The untrained eye will not understand that the unfrozen Cup B is actually colder than

---

[105] http://en.wikipedia.org/wiki/Mpemba_effect

the frozen Cup A. Furthermore, once Cup A nucleates, it begins pumping 'heat' energy into the freezer at 32°F which can further delay Cup B from nucleating.

These results won't always happen this way in a home environment, in part due to the stochastic nature of nucleation and in part due to other nucleation sites being present in both cups. In controlled lab conditions, the warmer water will freeze first 70% of the time or more depending on initial starting temps vs. freezer temps. Tweaking the conditions carefully can bring it to 90+%....part of the keys to the kingdom.

Tools and Sources

A List of Stuff You Probably Already Know You Need

It's completely possible and totally acceptable to produce craft cocktails using nothing more than a used Gatorade bottle (Page 15, in case you missed it). But, as you get more into the craft of mixing, you may find yourself craving nicer tools, if for no other reason than to look cool. Here are some recommendations, in no particular order.

- **Cocktail shaker**: before you buy it, try it. Some shakers stick or leak. Plastic is slightly better than metal because your hands won't get as cold.
- **Jigger/mini measuring cup**: Jiggers are designed to measure standard amounts quickly, whereas the OXO mini-measuring cup is more versatile. For a another surprisingly good option, search "OXO Mini Measuring Beaker Set"
- **Barspoon**: Make sure to get one with an 1/8-ounce bowl for measuring. Also good for stirring drinks, swizzling, and cracking ice.
- **Citrus Juicer**: The Amco Enameled Aluminum Lemon Squeezer works for both lemons and limes and satisfies a good balance between price and performance. Friends tell me some electronic juicers work very well, but I have not tried any.
- **Mini Conical Strainer**: For double-straining drinks and clarifying homemade ingredients. I prefer the RSVP conical version over the hemisphere-style made by OXO because it's easier to gently swirl the strainer to use more the mesh's surface area.
- **Vegetable peeler or paring knife**: The $4 Victorinox paring knife fits perfectly into your hand and stays sharp forever. A cheap and simple y-peeler makes a good alternative; the OXO version is a bit more durable, though better-suited to larger hands.
- **Channel Knife/Zester**: Once again, the OXO version is the gold standard here.
- **Pyrex measuring cup**: Useful for making batches of syrups and won't get messed up if you heat it. Also good for pouring stuff into bottles without a funnel.

A Few Less-Conventional Tools

- **Infrared and probe thermometers:** I use the small, dual-purpose Taylor Professional 9306 Thermometer. At $85, it isn't cheap, but it's incredibly useful and illuminating for both cooking and mixing.

- **AeroPress® Coffee filter:** Available everywhere for around $25. Good for extra-fine filtering and it also makes great coffee.

- **ISI Whipper:** A multitasker with its own chapter in this book.

- **ZeroWater filter:** The only water filter I know of that promises true zero total dissolved solids (TDS).

- **TDS Measure:** Many cheap, effective versions available. For confirming TDS.

- **pH Meter:** Generally difficult to use, easy to ruin, and require constant calibration. If you opt to use one, make sure to read up on pH, total titratable acid, and buy plenty of calibration fluid in at least two different pH's.

- **1-Micron filter bag:** I found the one I use on Amazon sold by a company called "Biodiesel Supply Store & Chemicals". Many different micron ratings are available.

- **Jewelry scale:** For measuring small amounts of modernist ingredients or powerful botanicals. Many types are available and most are cheap. I use one accurate to 0.01 grams with a max range of 100 grams. A calibration weight is helpful. **Weighing boats** are available at Modernist Pantry, though I've found a paper muffin cup works just as well.

- **Kitchen scale:** Get one that measures in both metric and English units and has a pull-out display. I use the $50 OXO version.

- **Atomizer:** Used for spraying flavors onto the tops of cocktails. I found mine from men's shaving supply store QED USA.

- **Dropper bottles:** I found mine on Amazon; Carey Nershi recommends the online store Specialty Bottle.

- **SodaStream:** Widely available at stores that sell housewares. The various models all work on the same principle, despite the widely differing designs. I recommend grabbing a few 0.5L-sized bottles for carbonating small amounts of ingredients. For the aquarium tubing used for the wine-carbonation trick, search for "Elite Silicone Airline Tubing for Aquarium" on Amazon.

- **Small coke bottles:** For rebottling easily oxidized ingredients. Available... everywhere.

- **Ice Molds:** Tovolo makes the 1" and 2" cube and 2" sphere silicone molds which serve as the gold standard for home enthusiasts. I've also had good luck with Japanese-style plastic ice sphere molds. They can impart a slight silicone off-taste. If this bothers you, take the finished cubes out, dunk them in a bin of very cold water (warm water causes the ice to crack) then store in the freezer until use.
- **Sous Vide Materials:** I've listed all the sources and details in the chapter "How to Infuse 200x Faster with Precision Temperature Control."
- **Essential Oils and Hydrosols:** The cheapest places to get these appear to be specialty and gourmet markets. Look under "aromatherapy." I bought a starter pack through Amazon, but I could probably have gotten the individual bottles cheaper a la carte at a brick and mortar store. Hydrosols are available at Rose Mountain Herbs.
- **Herbs, Botanicals, and Spices:** See the following section.
- **Modernist Ingredients:** See the following section as well as my "Guide to Scientific Ingredients" at the Science Fare blog.
- **Nut Milk Bag:** Used for non-messy filtration of plant matter. Available online at webstore Vermont Fiddle Heads.

Online Storefronts

As craft cocktails have become more mainstream, ingredients and tools have become increasingly available at mainstream retailers like Amazon. But some specialty shops are still worth visiting. Here are some of my recommendations.

- **Bevmo:** Large spirits distributor with good prices and selection. Popular on the west coast of the United States.
- **The Boston Shaker:** A Somerville, MA-based small business that carries all manner of specialty cocktail equipment, from edible hibiscus flowers to fine glassware. An awesome place—make an in-person visit someday if you can.
- **Dandelion Botanical Company:** Recommended by Carey Nershi as a source for botanicals used in making bitters.
- **DrinkUpNY:** Plenty of places online ship spirits, but DrinkUpNY stands out for their excellent selection of obscure ingredients and lenient shipping policy (they ship to some states other businesses will not ship to).

- **Kegworks:** General assortment of bar accessories, including cocktail bitters. Although bitters are more widely available now, Kegworks deserves credit for being one of the early online distributors of cocktail bitters.
- **Modernist Pantry:** Small quantities of Modernist ingredients (like emulsifiers, alternative acids, and hydrocolloids) for $5-$10 a package, with fast shipping.
- **Molecular Recipes:** Complete recipes, beautifully photographed, made with the exact ingredients you can buy at their storefront.
- **Mountain Rose Herbs:** A wide range of high quality bulk herbs, extracts, and even dropper bottles needed to experiment with bitters.
- **My Spice Sage:** Huge assortment of spices, good prices, useful search engine and categorization scheme.
- **Specialty Bottle:** Another recommendation from Carey. A source for bottles, from mason jars to 1 oz. dropper bottles.

An Annotated Bibliography for the Deeply Curious

Looking for cocktail books or blogs with plenty of recipes? There's a separate chapter for those, under "Find the Cocktail Recipes You Really Want." A constantly-updated wiki for resources is also posted on the companion blog to this book.

Note: Here I've only listed the resources that I found to be most useful when researching this book. There are many other great resources in each category, but I can't recommend what I haven't tried. This section will also be posted to the companion blog to this book and updated with reader comments.

Food Science in General

I would be lost without <u>On Food and Cooking</u> by Harold McGee. Nearly thirty years after its first printing, it remains one of the most useful resources I own. Anyone who's serious about food or drink should read it cover-to-cover. Another fantastic resource has been the massive 5-volume "book" that is <u>Modernist Cuisine</u>. Huge amounts of information are available within, though the hefty price tag can be hard to swallow. Try to find it at a library.

I've enjoyed paging through Robert Wolke's <u>What Einstein Told His Cook</u> series for light reading. Jeff Potter's popular <u>Cooking for Geeks</u> combines deep science with awesome at-home projects and recipes. For a book with lots of science, but focused more on deliciousness than anything else, see Aki Kamozawa and Alex Talbot's <u>Ideas in Food: Great Recipes and Why They Work</u>.

I can't leave out Joachim, Schloss, and Handel's <u>Science of Good Food</u>. The book is massive and totally underrated. A great supplement and reference book. For a much more technical publication, check out the multi-volume <u>Handbook of Food Science, Technology, and Engineering</u>, edited by Y. H. Hui. This is one to find in a library. Finally, keep up-to-date on modern research in gastronomy in <u>The Kitchen as Laboratory</u> by Cesar Vega's (with appearances from many others involved in ongoing research). For more papers like those featured in Vega's book see the open-access journal *Flavour* .

Sensory Analysis and Flavor Perception

If I had to choose one book to read in this category, it would be Chandler Burr's Emperor of Scent. He explains the science and importance of aroma with in an incredibly succinct and compelling voice. I'd also recommend Barb Stuckey's Taste: What You're Missing for a thorough overview of taste science and Gordon Shepher's Neurogastronomy, though the latter is a little bit dry. Worth skimming. For an easy-to-read book on neuroscience, see Jonah Lehrer's How We Decide.

Flavor Chemistry

Once again, Emperor of Scent is the best resource for understanding how chemicals translate into taste experiences in our minds. For more on scent, see Perfume, by Jean-Claude Ellena or the hard-to-find Perfumery: Practice and Principles by Calkin and Jellinek.

If you can find a copy to browse, the latest version of Fenaroli's Handbook of Flavor Ingredients makes a really eye-opening introduction to the vast body of knowledge the industry already has on flavors and their constituents. For home cooks, it's probably easier to start with The Flavor Bible by Karen Page and Andrew Dornenburg. No mention of aldehydes and esters here, just a list of what ingredients go with each other, as voted on by actual chefs.

Finally, a few other papers and books are mentioned in the chapter "Tinctures, Oils, and Extracts." These are mostly lists of flavors and compounds geared toward the technical crowd, but might be a useful starting point for more in-depth research.

Water and Ice

The easiest to read book in this category is Mariana Gosnell's Ice: The Nature, the History, and the Uses of an Astonishing Substance. Some other good books relevant to ice: The Chemical Physics of Ice by N. H. Fletcher and Frozen Food Science and Technology by Judith Evans. For water stuff, nothing beats Philip R. Ashurst and Robert Hargitt's Soft drink and fruit juice problems solved. It's a technical publication that's surprisingly easy to read. Finally, some topics specific to water that might be interesting to some can be found in <u>Technology of Bottle Water</u>, Third Edition, by Nicholas Dege.

Citrus

To answer the questions I posed about citrus, I used a handful of journal papers, several of them dating from decades ago. The specifics are referenced in the Citrus chapter. For useful reviews of modern citrus research, see <u>Citrus Fruit Biology, Technology, and Evaluation</u> by Milind Ladaniya and the <u>Handbook of Fruits and Fruit Processing</u>, edited by Y. H. Hui.

Food Preservation

Food preservation depends heavily on the specific food, processing techniques, storage conditions, and desired end quality. Search for papers addressing your specific topic. For a decent overview, see <u>Food Preservation Techniques</u>, edited by Peter Zeuthen and Leif Bøgh-Sørensen. Also enlightening is <u>The Art of Fermentation</u> by Sandor Katz. To find out about the safety of additives, I referenced <u>A Consumer's Dictionary of Food Additives</u>, 7th Edition, by Ruth Winter.

Modernist/Molecular Ingredients

<u>Modernist Cuisine</u> covers how to apply almost all the untraditional ingredients used by chefs today, but it's not very accessible due to its price. Jeff Potter covers a bunch in <u>Cooking for Geeks</u>, but few recipes are included. The best collection of recipes for the price remains Martin Lersch's <u>Texutre—A Hydrocolloid Recipe Collection</u>, available for free through khymos.org.

For more specific information about ingredients, see Ferran Adrià's <u>Modern Gastronomy: A to Z</u>, the more-technical <u>Handbook of Hydrocolloids</u>, Second Edition, edited by Phillips and Williams, or my own guide to scientific ingredients at ScienceFare.org.

Topical Books about Alcohol

You can't really appreciate classic cocktails without reading a little history. The most enjoyable book in this group has to be Eric Felten's <u>How's Your Drink?: Cocktails, Culture, and the Art of Drinking Well</u>. It's one of the few cocktail books I read cover to cover and couldn't put down. Some great insights can also be drawn from Brad Thomas Parsons' Bitters: A Spirited History of a Classic Cure-All and Darcy O'Neil's Fix the Pumps. Both gents explore fascinating uncharted territory and include dozens of useful recipes in their books.

Finally, some interesting insights can be drawn from these actual history books: Drink: a Cultural History by Iain Gately and The Spirits of America, A Social History of Alcohol by Eric Burns.

Wine Chemistry

I ended up cutting out a lot of information about wine and aromatized wine production from this book because I didn't feel my experiments were ready for primetime, but I will point out these useful references: Wine Chemistry and Biochemistry, edited by Victoria Moreno-Arribas and Carmen Polo, Introduction to Wine Laboratory Practices and Procedures by Jean Jacobson, and anything written by Maynard Amerine, particularly the 1980 edition of The Technology of Wine Making, which discusses aromatized wines more in-depth than more recent works. For more on vermouths, see The Mixellany Guide to Vermouth & Other Apéritifs by Jared Brown and Anistatia Miller.

Distillation

I've omitted distillation from this book because I didn't feel any of my exploration into it was ready to be published. But if you're interested (and you should be), see The Compleat Distiller by Nixon and McCaw and Whisky Technology, Production and Marketing, edited by Russell, Stewart, and Bamforth. Those two books should cover the vast majority of what you need to know about distilling, though they do not provide step-by-step directions for home application, for better or worse.

Acknowledgments

Thank you to the original **observation gastrophysicists** John, Mike, and Naveen for teaching me about cocktails and inspiring me to explore "the finer aspects of life." To the team at **Science Fare** Alex, Carolyn, Kevin, and Naveen (again) I am grateful because without you guys, I'd just be talking to myself.

I've been floored by the generosity and knowledge of **bartenders** like Andrew, Darcy, Dushan, Gaby, Giles, Gus, Jeff, Mattias, Pip, Stephen, as well as other **creatives** like Camper, Carey, Chandlerr, Eva, Fred, Jimmy, John J., and Sebastian. Thank you all for giving me a peek into your world.

This book would be much shorter if not for the time of all the **scientists and experts** who agreed to speak with me. Thank you guys and gals. And it would be much harder to read if not for the effort of my **"beta-testers"** Charlene, Elizabeth, Jesse, Mark, Neil, Rukesh, and Sam, with a special nod to Carey.

And to you, dear second-person protagonist reader, thanks for buying this book. I sincerely hope you found it useful.

Cheers!

Contact Information

Updates, errata, and new content will be posted at
http://www.craftcocktailsathome.com

For any issues regarding the content, publication, or distribution of this book, the single point of contact is the author, at kevin@craftcocktailsathome.com

Colophon

The original source for this book was created in Microsoft Word 2010 and saved as a PDF with Adobe Acrobat Professional. Illustrations were designed with Microsoft Powerpoint and drawn by *illustrador* from the fiverr® marketplace. Images were processed with Adobe Photoshop. Technical figures, unless otherwise specified, were produced by the author with Microsoft Excel.

The fonts in this book are Adobe Garamond Pro and Century Gothic.

Book layout by the author.

Cover Design by *Neilko73* on 99designs.

About the Author

Kevin Liu started writing about food and science online at ScienceFare.org in 2011. He doesn't plan to stop anytime soon.

Made in the USA
Lexington, KY
18 December 2015